YES, YOU CAN!

Other Books by the Authors

By Sam Deep and Lyle Sussman
Smart Moves
Smart Moves for People in Charge
What to Say to Get What You Want
What to Ask When You Don't Know What to Say
Speaking Skills for Bankers
COMEX: The Communication Experience in Human Relations

By Sam Deep
Human Relations in Management
A Program of Exercises for Management and Organizational Behavior, with
    James A. Vaughan
Introduction to Business: A Systems Approach, with William D. Brinkloe
Current Perspectives for Managing Organizations, with Bernard M. Bass
Studies in Organizational Psychology, with Bernard M. Bass

By Lyle Sussman
Communication for Supervisors and Managers, with Paul D. Krivonos
Increasing Supervisory Effectiveness, with Frank Kuzmits and
    Richard Herden

YES, YOU CAN!

1,200 Inspiring Ideas for
Work, Home, and Happiness

SAM DEEP & LYLE SUSSMAN

ADDISON-WESLEY PUBLISHING COMPANY

Reading, Massachusetts   Menlo Park, California   New York
Don Mills, Ontario   Wokingham, England
Amsterdam   Bonn   Sydney   Singapore   Tokyo   Madrid
San Juan   Paris   Seoul   Milan   Mexico City   Taipei

Library of Congress Cataloging-in-Publication Data

Deep, Samuel D.
    Yes, you can! : 1200 inspiring ideas for work, home, and happiness / Sam Deep and Lyle Sussman.
        p. cm.
    ISBN 0-201-47965-6
    1. Success. 2. Life skills—Handbooks, manuals, etc. 3. Social skills. I. Sussman, Lyle, 1944–   II. Title.
BF637.S8D367 1996
158—dc20   95-40695
                                                                                                        CIP

First edition published by Seminars by Sam Deep, November 1993

Cover design by Suzanne Heiser
Text design by Janis Owens
Set in 11-point Adobe Garamond by Wellington Graphics, Westwood, MA

3 4 5 6 7 8 9 10-DOH-0099989796
Third printing, November 1996

*We wish for the reader of this book the **courage**
to discover the need for personal change,
the **wisdom** to find the right path to it,
the **power** to bring it about, and
the **love** to make others a part of it.*

Contents

Chapter 1: Think Positively

Chapter 2: Act Powerfully

Chapter 3: Communicate Effectively

Chapter 4: Build Relationships

Chapter 5: Motivate Others

Chapter 6: Prosper at Work

Chapter 7: Prosper at Home

To the Reader

We had one goal in writing **_Yes, You Can!_**—to create the most vital book you've ever owned.

You can use it to succeed in all phases of life—thinking, doing, speaking, listening, planning, managing, leading, working, parenting, loving, serving, and much more. The proven suggestions in this book will help you in your professional as well as your personal life.

This book contains 125 "advisements," each on a separate page headed by a goal (for example, "Increase your job security.") followed by an explanation of why that goal is important. Below each advisement is a list of anywhere from six to fifteen actions that can help you achieve the stated goal.

The advisements are introduced by memorable sayings. Many were uttered by famous personalities. Some of the quoted authors lived in ancient times; many are with us today. Some quotations are witty; others are dead serious. A few jump right out at you; others require thought. _All_ put you in a frame of mind that helps you profit from the book.

Our preparation for the writing of **_Yes, You Can!_** came in many forms. Our formal education, reading, teaching, and consulting played the roles you'd expect. But the main source of the benefit we hope you'll find in this book has been life itself. Together we have spent over a hundred years making mistakes and experiencing success—at work and at home—and watching others do the same. That experience has been our primary research for this book.

— *Sam Deep and Lyle Sussman*

How to Use This Book

Most books are meant to be read. ***Yes, You Can!*** was written to be *used.*

We hope you will find the advisements too valuable to look at only once before placing the book on your bookshelf. We hope you'll use them repeatedly to get better results throughout your life.

Here is how we suggest you do this:

First: Enjoy the book.
Have fun checking out some of the great quotes. Skim through the pages at random; look for bits of advice you can use immediately. Read the entire book through if you're a "cover-to-cover" reader. Share it with your friends, colleagues, and loved ones.

Second: Find the advice you need.
Shop through the table of contents for the advisements that are most likely to offer the skill-building suggestions of greatest value to you. Highlight the titles of the advisements on which you'll focus. Then dig into the advice they contain. Circle the bullets in front of the three or four suggestions that make the most sense to you. As you study these items, take notes in the white space of the facing page. Jot down any insights that will help you when you begin to apply the recommendations.

Third: Set priorities.
On the table of contents, rank the titles of the advisements you have studied from most to least essential and from most to least urgent. Identify the first one you want to work on.

Fourth: Go to work.
Plan to spend a month working on each advisement. Turn to the page of your highest ranked advisement, at the top of the page write the date that is exactly one month from your starting date. Enter the end date and the title of the advisement in your appointment calendar. You've just set your first personal development goal for *Yes, You Can!*

Next, start doing what the advice suggests. Begin with the recommendation that looks best to you, and work through the list.

When a month has passed and you've made progress, turn to the advisement you ranked second. Continue this process over the coming months until you have addressed each advisement of importance to you. Every six months or so stop to take stock of your accomplishments and celebrate them.

Fifth: Attend the *Yes, You Can!* Program.
At any point during your use of this book you might profit from attending a *Yes, You Can!* program. This event is led by the authors for individuals who want to derive maximum value from the counsel contained in the book. We offer this program in approximately fifty U.S. cities each year. It can also be brought to your company. See the back of the book for more information.

YES, YOU CAN!

CHAPTER 1

THINK POSITIVELY

Change your thoughts and you change your world.

—NORMAN VINCENT PEALE

You can't lead a cavalry charge
if you think you look funny on
a horse.

—JOHN PEERS

Increase your self-esteem.

People with low self-esteem rarely achieve their potential. They won't take necessary risks, they wallow in self-blame, they can't trust others, and they remain in the background when they are needed up front. Can you elevate your self-worth?

Yes, You Can!
⊰⊱

֍ Get angry enough to do what it takes to reverse the losses you suffer as a result of your low self-regard. Don't tolerate another awful day of the status quo.

֍ If you hold deep-seated spiritual beliefs, fall back on them. Many religions provide believers with an inner power that builds self-esteem.

֍ Elevate other human beings. Teach them something to improve their lives. Serve them. Help them achieve goals they can't reach by themselves. Empower them to succeed. Watch your inner self grow as a result.

֍ Write down three personal development goals. At the beginning of each day ask yourself, "What will I do to work on one of my goals today?" Let the pursuit and the achievement of these goals lift your self-concept.

֍ Make a list of your most important accomplishments in the past twelve months. Study the list. None of them may get into *The Guinness Book of Records*, but you *have* made a difference in the lives of others.

֍ Talk about your low self-esteem to someone whose opinion you respect. Get ready for a shock when this person tells you how valuable you are.

֍ Write an essay that answers these questions: What life experiences have led you to devalue yourself? What price do you pay for feeling the way you do—how much does it hold you back? Are you angry enough about what is going on to wG19ant to make a change? What's your plan? When will you start?

Think Positively

When it is dark enough, you
can see the stars.

—RALPH WALDO EMERSON

Feel more optimistic.

We live in increasingly negative times fueled by the disintegration of social bonds and the dissolution of religious faith. A measure of optimism helps to combat gloom and gives us the courage and the energy to shed adversity. Can you muster hopefulness in the midst of despair?

Yes, You Can!

୧୭

- Remember that life teaches us that *this, too, will pass.*

- Dispute thoughts that a present adversity is hopeless or permanent. Describe the causes of your pessimism on a sheet of paper; next to each cause, document the evidence that it is real and not imagined. For each real cause, write down at least one way to counteract it. Challenge the imagined causes with alternative explanations and contradictory evidence.

- Share your concerns with people you love. Talk through problems with them. Let them help you.

- Reject unnecessarily negative assumptions. *Example:* Rather than believe that the world is falling apart, tell yourself, "We would benefit from a moral renewal."

- When you feel yourself slipping, talk yourself out of despair. Say something like, "I'm going to overwhelm this bad feeling. Optimism is pouring in through every pore of my skin."

- Recognize that two common causes of pessimism are fear and hate. The greatest danger of these emotions is that they shut off your mind. Determine whether either is at the root of your discouragement, and if you discover one of these emotions, exorcise it.

- Distract yourself from depressing thoughts. Every time you catch yourself complaining, quickly immerse yourself in an activity that will take your mind off the troubling subject.

- Keep bleak news in perspective.

*We should all be concerned
about the future because we
will have to spend the rest of
our lives there.*

—Charles F. Kettering

Look to the future, and forget the past.

One of the reasons some people never have happy todays is that they continue to relive unhappy yesterdays. They would rather revisit the pain of the past than plan for a fantastic future. You can't change what has already happened to you. You *can* get on with your life, and you can put safeguards into place to ensure a better tomorrow.

Yes, You Can!
&

§ If the pain in your history is emotionally devastating (for example, sexual abuse), get professional help immediately rather than relying on the following advice.

§ Write a plan for what you will do to make certain that the sadness in your history doesn't return. If preventing a recurrence is not totally within your control, whom will you enlist to help?

§ Picture your memory as a roll of photographic film. The past represents film already exposed—some of the poses may not be your favorites. The future is the unexposed portion awaiting images you have yet to experience. What wonderful memories do you intend to capture on the remaining frames?

§ Whenever you feel yourself slipping into the negatives of the past, slam a pillow, snap your fingers, or shout, "No!" Use a strong physical signal as an on-off switch.

§ Say this and mean it: "At some point in my life I have to give up all hope for a better yesterday."

§ Tell yourself, "Today is the first day of the rest of my life."

§ Ask a loved one, "What can I begin doing today that would make it more fun for you to be with me?"

§ Ask someone at work, "What can I begin doing today that would allow me to serve you better?"

When I look back on all these
worries I remember the story
of the old man who said on his
deathbed that he had had a lot
of trouble in his life, most of
which never happened.

—WINSTON CHURCHILL

Reduce your worry.

How do you handle your worries? Do you keep them in perspective, or do you allow them to discourage, depress, and debilitate you? You can prevent your worries from making more worries.

Yes, You Can!

§ Ask yourself, "Is it real? What is the evidence that there really is something to fear?"

§ If the situation is real, what are the implications? How long will it last? How will you deal with it? Is it something you can change—right now?

§ Ask yourself, "What do I accomplish by worrying about this?" If the feared event is in the future, ask yourself three questions: "What is the worst thing that could happen? How likely is this possibility? What can I do to reduce the probability that it will occur?"

§ *Carpe Diem!* (Seize the day!) Act now to keep this situation from taking you over.

§ Ask yourself, "How will I feel about this a year from now? Will the test of time show that this is anywhere near as important as I've convinced myself it is?"

§ Change how you foresee a dreaded event. Discover what is actually *good* in it and look forward to those benefits.

§ Talk over your problems with someone who will listen.

§ Write about your problems. Jot down some ideas for how to deal with your problems.

§ Promise people you know that whenever they catch you worrying about things that are beyond your control, you'll pay them $1. Agree to see a therapist as soon as you've lost $10.

§ Read Dale Carnegie's book *How to Stop Worrying and Start Living.*

Constant effort and frequent mistakes are the stepping stones to genius.

—ELBERT HUBBARD

Forgive your mistakes.

Some people live in a perpetual state of penance. They repeatedly suffer the pain of their errors, fearing the future because they are paralyzed by the past. Can you remove the shackles of your past mistakes and move forward?

Yes, You Can!
⚬

§ When you've made an error that gets you down, take out a sheet of paper and write down exactly what happened.

§ Assess *why* you made the mistake. What were the causes? How many of them were within your control?

§ Think about the problems or pain created by the error and who might suffer. What's the worst thing likely to happen as a result? Check with someone else; reality usually isn't as bad as your fears would have you believe.

§ Apologize and seek forgiveness quickly from people who may have suffered as a result of your mistake. When they offer forgiveness, accept it with thanks.

§ If your guilt is consuming you, seek professional guidance or spiritual counsel.

§ Recognize the benefits of the mistake. What good has come out of it? If nothing else, you have learned a valuable lesson for your future behavior. What is it? (Vulcanized rubber, Post-it notes, and penicillin were all created by mistake.)

§ Use your mistakes to build a greater understanding of others who make mistakes and how they feel about them. Forgive generously and quickly when you believe that the other person is sincerely repentant.

§ Remember that a mistake reflects your performance in a particular situation under a particular set of circumstances. It is not a statement about you. You have the power to change your performance in the future.

*Problems are only
opportunities in work clothes.*

—Henry J. Kaiser

Conquer adversity.

Everyone goes through bad times. Successful people know how to snap back. Can you develop the qualities that will enable you to triumph over adversity?

Yes, You Can!

❦

- ⸙ Maintain confidence in your resilience. Don't underestimate your power to push beyond what you're normally capable of. Take advantage of this opportunity to prove that you can take control of your life.

- ⸙ Pray. Develop an unshakable belief in something greater than yourself. Faith in God is a great comfort in times of trial. Even people who aren't religious need to believe in something beyond self-preservation.

- ⸙ Move quickly through the natural period of feeling sorry for yourself. Dissolve your disappointment, anger, or grief so you can get on with your life.

- ⸙ Develop a concrete plan for recovery soon after adversity strikes. Win the battle by committing yourself to an aggressive strategy for overcoming hardship.

- ⸙ Find the opportunity that adversity always presents. Any change in the status quo provides an opening for improving your life. For example, after losing a job you may discover a lucrative career opportunity that you might never have pursued from within the comfort of steady employment.

- ⸙ Let your friends and family help to absorb the pain and give you ideas to cope with the adversity and get beyond it. Don't pull in—reach out.

- ⸙ Persist. Fight. Survive. Don't even *think* about quitting.

- ⸙ Fulfill the obligation you have to yourself and to the people in your life not to even *consider* the possibility of allowing yourself to be victimized by tough times.

Our life is what our thoughts make it.

—MARCUS AURELIUS

Think clearly.

Errors in thinking cause us to erect roadblocks in our minds that prevent us from properly weighing decisions. You can get past these roadblocks.

Yes, You Can!

❧

- Wait as long as you can to draw conclusions about anything. Remain open to the certainty that someone has additional information on the subject that is worth listening to. Don't be so quick to dismiss ideas that contradict what you already know.

- Divorce the message from the messenger. Don't evaluate information according to how you feel about who's delivering it.

- Don't be seduced into believing that phenomena are causally linked simply because they are statistically related. *Example:* Cities with many churches usually also harbor large numbers of prostitutes because large urban centers tend to spawn both, not because one causes the other.

- Don't be too quick to form explanations for the behavior of others, for results in data you collect, or for events you observe. An after-the-fact interpretation is rarely correct if you lack a thorough knowledge of the circumstances unique to, for example, that person, data, or event.

- Reject slogans, propaganda, and buzzwords intended to short-circuit your thinking. *Example:* How much of what is advertised as "free" doesn't cost anything?

- Sleep on major decisions. Time has a way of clarifying thinking.

- Don't stereotype. Not all snakes are poisonous; not all chemical companies pollute; not all lawyers are just in it for the money.

- Don't assume that the first bit of information you get on any new subject is correct; continue to listen, read, and ask.

Have more than thou showest;
speak less than thou knowest.

—WILLIAM SHAKESPEARE

Prevent cockiness.

Self-confidence is an empowering belief: it encourages us to take risks, it enables us to act decisively, and it spurs us on to achieve our full potential. But when your successes cause you to be seduced by your press clippings, you may cross the line from surety to self-obsession. You can protect yourself from a case of conceit.

Yes, You Can!
※

- As soon as you think you're pretty hot stuff, examine a globe or world map. There are 5 billion people on the planet. How many of them know your name?

- Cockiness is often little more than camouflage for self-doubt. Ask yourself what insecurities you're compensating for by pumping up your ego.

- Recognize that your talents are a gift. What people admire is nothing more than God acting through you.

- Rid your language of self-serving statements and self-promotion. Cut your *I* statements in half. Mention accomplishments only when others insist that you do so.

- Spend more time listening. You can't boast when you're not talking.

- When others recognize your successes, don't feign modesty and don't explain your accomplishments. Just say "thank you." *Do* acknowledge those who have helped you.

- Study the behavior of the most talented and respected people in your profession. Model your behavior after the classy way they handle their fame.

- If you're not sure whether you're becoming vain, ask trusted colleagues, friends, or family members this question: "What one behavior do you see in me that might be construed by others as conceit?"

The desire of perfection is the worst disease that ever afflicted the human mind.

—LOUIS MARQUIS DE FONTANES

Accept imperfection in yourself.

There's nothing wrong with striving to be the best; in fact, it's a winning attitude. It's *very* wrong to expect others and yourself to be flawless under all conditions. If you do so, you are asking for nothing but frustration, because consistent perfection is impossible. Can you learn to tolerate less than perfection in yourself?

Yes, You Can!

≪∞≫

- ♦ Draw a line down the center of a sheet of paper. In the left column enter "The Pleasures of Perfectionism." In the right column jot down drawbacks under the heading "The Pain of Perfectionism." Which side has more potent points?

- ♦ Go back over the pleasure/pain sheet. Reevaluate the validity of each entry on the pleasure side to make certain that it isn't simply a means of avoiding risk, maintaining control, or protecting your ego.

- ♦ Ask other perfectionists about the pain and pleasure *they* experience from such behavior.

- ♦ Ask people close to you how your perfectionism affects them, your relationship with them, and you.

- ♦ Identify three aspects of your life that you love but that you've ignored lately because you've been trying so hard to succeed. Vow to bring them back into your life.

- ♦ Take stock of your achievements. Marvel at how far you've progressed, rather than lamenting over the degree to which you've fallen short of perfection.

- ♦ Do something wild and crazy. Don't plan it, don't have any expectations about it, and don't evaluate the results.

- ♦ Concentrate on the here and now; don't obsess about the past and what you *might* have accomplished.

- ♦ Embrace quality as a *journey*. You may never achieve the goal of perfection, but you can have a marvelous trip!

A cynic is a man who, when he smells flowers, looks around for a coffin.

—H. L. MENCKEN

Be less cynical.

A cynic goes through life both depressed and depressing. Most people have enough negativity in their lives without having to add yours to their load. They won't tolerate someone who smells roses and looks around for a casket. If you *want* to improve your outlook on life, you can do it.

Yes, You Can!

※

- If your cynicism turns into clinical depression, seek professional counsel. Signs of depression are a loss of interest in work, family, or fun; insomnia or excessive sleep; overeating or loss of appetite; acute sorrow or plunging self-esteem; and fatigue.

- Consider the impact of your negative attitude on people around you. It may prevent them from doing their best and living their lives fully. If you have negative people in *your* life, avoid contact with them until you are strong enough to deflect their pessimism.

- Rent the video *It's a Wonderful Life*. Watch it and answer this question: "Suppose you had never been born, how many lives would be less complete because you are not around?"

- Read the book *The Miracle Worker*. After you've read it, answer this question: "What can I do to start 'hearing' and 'seeing' the things Helen Keller heard and saw?"

- Observe others who've achieved the success you hope to attain. Notice how many of them are positive and enthusiastic people. Do you think they became that way *following* success, or do you think their optimism is one of the big reasons *for* their achievements?

- Talk to professionals who devote their lives to helping people with grief and sorrow—for example people who work in pediatric oncology. Where do they get the strength to get up each day and attack their jobs? You'll likely find that the key to their motivation is hope—without it you're dead.

If you think you can, you can.
If you think you can't,
you're right.

—Mary Kay Ash

Avoid negative self-talk.

What you see in your mind is what you create; what you think about is what you get; and what you speak is what you become. You can maintain a high-quality mental outlook that rejects the thoughts and the language that hold you back.

Yes, You Can!

❧

§ Replace the phrase "I'll try" with "I will." "I'll try" means "I feel compelled to do it, but I really don't want to do it." A try is nothing more than that.

§ Ask fewer questions that start with the word *why*. *Example:* Change "Why do you disagree?" to "What do you disagree with?" Notice how much less nagging and more assertive the second question is.

§ Kill *should*'s, *could*'s, *ought*'s, and *have to*'s. These words increase your stress and your guilt. *Example:* Replace "I should pay the bills tonight" with "I will [want to] pay the bills tonight."

§ Start saying yes when people offer to help you, instead of responding automatically, "No thanks, I can handle it."

§ Start accepting compliments and praise graciously instead of protesting that you don't deserve them. Say a big "thank you" and nothing more.

§ When asked how you feel (even gratuitously), say, "Great" or "Marvelous," not just "Fine" or "Okay."

§ Stop mumbling. Speak clearly, distinctly, and confidently.

§ Open up your future possibilities by replacing "I can't," "I don't," or "I won't" with "I haven't up until now."

§ Never say, "I'm too [stupid, fat, short, inexperienced, weak, afraid, disorganized] to. . . ."

§ Never say or think, "I might fail." You might learn a new way *not* to do something, but you'll never fail.

Hating people is like burning
down your house to get rid of
a rat.

—HARRY EMERSON FOSDICK

Stop holding grudges.

Life lets us down. People we count on disappoint us; others transgress against us. A financial fortune is lost overnight; a healthy body is broken in an instant. When misfortune strikes, some people generate enormous resentment against others or against life in general; they are determined to extract some measure for what they have lost. Others accept their fate and go on to make the best of life. You can free yourself of grudges.

Yes, You Can!

❧

- ❧ Recognize that the grudge is weighing you down and holding you back. Even if you recapture what you've lost, you'll only regain the status quo. Use your precious time, instead, to grow and to advance.

- ❧ Don't allow misfortune to turn you into an entitlement seeker. Instead of focusing on your rights and what you have coming to you, aim for the higher things in life. Help others out of fixes like yours; accomplish an extraordinary feat; acquire knowledge; leave behind a meaningful legacy.

- ❧ Talk to others about what has happened to you. Each time you rehash the scenario, take one additional measure of rancor out of your voice. Eventually you'll reach the point where you can honestly laugh at your fate.

- ❧ Ask people whom you trust for one example of dysfunction they see in your behavior as a result of a grudge you carry around. Once you have put this behavior behind you, ask them to suggest another self-defeating behavior to work on.

- ❧ Visualize the troubling event(s). Reduce the size of the picture by moving it away from you. Make it as small as you can. Each time you do this, start with a smaller picture, and you'll eventually be free of it.

- ❧ Forgive publicly any persons who may have wronged you. Get on with your life.

CHAPTER 2

ACT & POWERFULLY

Forty thousand wishes won't fill your bucket with fishes.

—FISHERMAN'S SAYING

*Success in life comes not from
holding a good hand, but in
playing a poor hand well.*

—WARREN G. LESTER

Achieve success.

Everyone wants to succeed, even though we cannot all agree on a definition of *success*. Whatever your definition, you can depend on a proven formula for getting what you want from life.

Yes, You Can!

૭

- ৡ The first step toward success is to become totally fed up at not having achieved it yet. Get impatient that you haven't reached your life goals.

- ৡ Decide on exactly what you want. Where do you yearn to be in life? What will success look, sound, smell, feel, and taste like when you achieve it?

- ৡ Map out your plan for success. What will you do? By when? With whom? Using what new resources?

- ৡ Take action! Do it! Follow through with *passion*. Stay physically fit and build your energy.

- ৡ As you implement your plan, pay back those who help you succeed.

- ৡ Spend five minutes each day improving the quality of your communication with others.

- ৡ Believe in yourself and persist. Abraham Lincoln lost eight elections before becoming president. Colonel Sanders suffered 1,000 rejections before he sold his first chicken recipe.

- ৡ Respond to the feedback you get as you implement your plan. Learn from what happens at each stage. Adjust and succeed.

- ৡ Imitate people who have accomplished goals like yours. Do what they do; say what they say; think what they think.

- ৡ Don't be afraid to fail—Abe and the Colonel weren't—and don't be afraid to succeed.

- ৡ Serve; give others more than they expect; help them without reservation; be a team player.

With your talents and industry, with science, and that steadfast honesty, which eternally pursues right, regardless of consequences, you may promise yourself everything but health, without which there is no happiness.

—THOMAS JEFFERSON

Improve your health.

Good health is a prerequisite for tackling each of the challenges in this book. No matter what your age or circumstances, you can improve your health in some simple ways.

Yes, You Can!

❧

§ Don't smoke. Even those who escape cancer have their energy sapped by this nasty habit. If you drink alcohol, use it responsibly. Excessive use causes accidents, illness, family trauma, and a deterioration of your personal effectiveness.

§ Don't use drugs. Substances like cocaine can damage the cardiovascular system.

§ Reduce your risk of AIDS and other sexually transmitted diseases through a combination of abstinence, fidelity, and the use of condoms.

§ Get a complete physical every two years before the age of forty and every year thereafter.

§ Wear a seat belt every time you drive.

§ Protect your skin from the sun. Be certain to get *enough* sun in the winter months to ward off depressed moods, lethargy, and increased appetite.

§ Eat three well-balanced meals each day. Cut down on fats. Watch your sodium intake. Eat more fruits, vegetables, and grains. Drink plenty of water. Shun food fads and diet plans.

§ Exercise regularly. Consult your physician before you start.

§ Have your drinking water analyzed for bacteria and lead.

§ Install at least one smoke alarm and one carbon dioxide detector in your home, and keep the batteries fresh. Check radon levels if you live in a high-risk area of the country.

§ Use your mind to improve your health. Better relationships and a more positive outlook on life will benefit your physical well-being. Even laughter helps!

Whenever the urge to exercise comes upon me, I lie down for a while and it passes.

—Robert Maynard Hutchins

Exercise wisely.

Nothing is more consistently prescribed by physicians for a healthy, energetic, and productive life than exercise. You can achieve these goals for yourself.

Yes, You Can!

❧

- Before getting started, see a doctor and set specific fitness goals.

- Don't become obsessed with exercise. Three twenty-minute aerobic workouts per week are enough for most people to stay physically fit.

- Don't expect immediate, magical results. Shoot for gradual, long-term progress. Don't punish yourself by swallowing the "no pain, no gain" philosophy. Listen to your body; don't push it past its limits.

- Walk briskly one mile a day after dinner. Walk down the hall to see a colleague instead of picking up the telephone. Park in remote, but *safe* sections of parking lots. Take the stairs for climbs of three flights or less.

- Before investing in expensive equipment, make a serious commitment to exercise. Research the relative benefits and drawbacks of treadmills, stationary bikes, cross-country ski machines, stair climbers, free weights, and multi-station gym machines.

- Choose an exercise you enjoy so you'll stick with it.

- Spend three to five minutes warming up your muscles and cardiovascular system before doing *any* exercise.

- The older you get, the more you need to supplement aerobic exercise with strength training, flexibility exercises, and weight-bearing activities, which help you keep your bones strong.

- During an aerobic workout, keep your heart rate at 60 to 80 percent of its predicted maximum rate for your age.

- Discontinue strenuous exercise during illness.

Energy, like the Biblical grain of mustard seed, will remove mountains.

—Hosea Ballou

Increase your energy.

One of the most severe limiting factors when you are working toward a better life is your level of energy. You can reduce the number of times you feel too tired to accomplish your goals.

Yes, You Can!

❧

- Schedule playful breaks into your workday: listen to a favorite song; plan a fun weekend or evening; browse through your favorite catalog; fantasize about your next vacation; play with a puzzle or toy; call your best friend; do something that you love to do.

- Eat a light lunch dominated by protein to ensure afternoon vigor.

- Drink plenty of water—at least eight glasses a day.

- Fill your diet with plenty of grains, fresh fruits, and vegetables.

- Laugh a lot. Hearty belly laughs stimulate the release of chemicals in the brain that increase well-being.

- Exercise briskly at least three times a week, for twenty minutes each session.

- Find a healthy pick-me-up that provides needed sugar to your system in midafternoon when most people's blood sugar drops.

- Make sure you do enough deep breathing during the day to keep sufficient oxygen in your blood. Three or four times during the day, take eight deep breaths and hold each one for a long time. Continue the deep breathing if you notice a difference in your energy level.

- If you get tired in the late afternoon, take a refreshing catnap.

- Get the right amount of sleep—you know you're on track when you can awake simultaneously with the ringing of your alarm clock.

Do not take life too seriously.
You will never get out of it
alive.

—ELBERT HUBBARD

Relax.

Life rushes on at a frenetic pace, and stress is all around you. The few moments you get to yourself each day may be the only opportunities you have to rest an overworked mind and body. You can learn how to relax.

Yes, You Can!

❧

- Cuddle up with a good book.

- Unwind with an enjoyable hobby. Collecting, crafting, and studying a favorite subject are reliable sources of diversion.

- Learn how to fantasize. Play with your mind. Dream dreams. Imagine situations you want to have happen.

- Take every day of vacation you have coming to you—in large chunks. When you return to work, say to yourself, "No one is going to mess with this good feeling for at least a week." Protect it for as long as you can.

- Don't plan how you'll use your leisure time. Just do the first fun thing that comes to mind.

- Spend time with children; let them teach you how to play again.

- Set aside at least one hour each day for yourself. Never do anything you *have* to do during that time. Spend it alone or with loved ones or with friends who have a knack for helping you to unwind.

- Find a space in your home where you can physically shut out the rest of the world for short but regular periods. Kick back and successively relax the muscle groups in your body. Start with your furrowed brow.

- Rent a video of the 1937 movie *Lost Horizon*.

- True inner peace comes from a permanent connection with God. Let Him into your life.

- Go on a spiritual retreat.

A man dies daily, only to be reborn in the morning, bigger, better, and wiser.

—EMMETT FOX

Defeat insomnia.

It's great to wake up refreshed in the morning, rather than be jolted out of a sound snooze because you couldn't get to sleep the night before. Sleep deprivation can bring serious consequences: irritability and fatigue, and susceptibility to a wide range of illnesses from headaches to psychosis. Like the average person, you can fall asleep within five to ten minutes.

Yes, You Can!

- Monitor your diet to ensure that you're not ingesting large amounts of caffeine within a few hours of retiring.

- Cut back on the pace of your physical activity at least one hour before retiring.

- Refuse to participate in any disturbing or stimulating discussions in the last hour before retiring for the night. Don't watch the news just before going to bed.

- Take a calming, satisfying book to bed. Get under the covers and read lying on your back.

- Play a relaxation tape at bedside. Some are recorded just for this purpose, or choose your own from the easy-listening section of your music store.

- Select a pleasant, satisfying fantasy to run through in your mind once the lights go out. Keep searching for one that works consistently for you.

- Don't think about going to sleep; focus on getting as cozy and as comfortable as you can in bed.

- After lying in bed for thirty minutes without falling asleep, get up and do something relaxing. Then return to bed for a fresh start.

- If your problem is serious, get an appointment at the sleep disorder clinic at the nearest medical center.

Archie doesn't know how to worry without gettin' upset.

—EDITH BUNKER IN "ALL IN THE FAMILY"

Reduce your stress.

We live incredibly hectic lives, doing more and more with less and less. You can defeat the resulting stress before it gets you.

Yes, You Can!
❦

- Engage in *active* leisure activities such as taking in amusement park rides, mountain climbing, skiing, playing tennis.

- Find a hobby that exercises and relaxes your mind. *Examples:* collecting, playing music, reading, painting, working on crafts.

- Set aside three hours each weekend to visit a local museum, library, or historic site.

- Redecorate your office: paint the walls a soothing blue; put a table lamp on your desk for easier reading; get a few green plants to provide visual pleasure; bring something from home to personalize the decor.

- Take frequent short breaks: inhale very slowly and deeply for five seconds, taking ten seconds to exhale; drink a full glass of water on each break.

- Take your vacations!

- Reject stress-generating thoughts. When you've been cut off in traffic, chuckle at the other driver's incompetence or selfishness rather than getting enraged. Replace catastrophic words like *awful, terrible,* and *horrendous* with phrases like "It could have been better." Stop expecting so much of yourself and others.

- Buy a book or a tape on relaxation techniques and breathing exercises. Find one that works for you.

- Practice good nutrition, get regular exercise, and adopt proper sleeping patterns.

- Before you buy any so-called labor-saving device (for example, a computer), be sure it will really make your life better and not merely cram more productivity into your day.

*If you don't know where you
are going, you might wind up
someplace else.*

—YOGI BERRA

Achieve personal goals.

Having personal goals establishes our hope for a better tomorrow; attaining them gives us a sense of satisfaction and accomplishment. You can set and achieve personal development goals.

Yes, You Can!
ॐ

§ Construct goals that are challenging and stretch your reach, but don't frustrate yourself by setting goals that you'll never accomplish. Limit yourself to three goals at a time.

§ Set goals with this question: "How will I add value to the people I serve (for example, customers), to the people who serve me (for example, employees), and to myself?"

§ Write down your goals. Put them in your time planner or in another visible place where you'll see them frequently. A thought-about goal is a wish; a written-down goal becomes a commitment.

§ Make your goals specific so that you can begin taking the exact steps needed to accomplish them. Replace "to go back to school" with "to enroll in the fall class of the business program at the community college."

§ Schedule each of the steps you need to take to accomplish the goal. Put them on a realistic timeline.

§ Visualize yourself achieving each goal. See, hear, smell, touch, and taste the doing of it.

§ Go public with your goals. Discuss them with others to increase your commitment to them.

§ Engage in frequent self-talk about your goals. Take stock of how well you're doing, and adjust your steps to get better results. Congratulate yourself on your successes. Prod yourself to overcome procrastination.

§ Whenever you achieve a personal development goal, celebrate and then go on to a new one.

Sixty years ago I knew everything; now I know nothing. Education is the progressive discovery of our own ignorance.

—WILL DURANT

Expand your knowledge.

There is no practical limit to the amount of information you can put into your brain. You can take advantage of its vast capacity to soak up knowledge by pursuing any topic that interests you. You can learn anything you want.

Yes, You Can!

∞

§ Set a personal development goal of gaining knowledge in a specific field on a particular topic. Go for it!

§ Spend time with well-educated people—especially those who like to talk about ideas. Don't be intimidated by them; listen to them, converse with them, and learn from them.

§ Ask lots of questions. When someone discusses something unfamiliar to you, ask him or her to explain. The only dumb question is the one you didn't ask.

§ Break out of the habit of watching TV or videos in the evening. See a play, attend a symphony, or go to a travel lecture.

§ Read nonfiction, biographies, newsmagazines, and newspapers. Carry reading material with you for when you can turn dead time into learning time, even if only for a few minutes.

§ Keep a collection of educational audiotapes in your car to make commuting and travel more profitable.

§ Continue your formal education. Sign up for a college course, a class at your library, or a seminar at work.

§ If you can afford to travel, visit a different destination each time.

§ Every Sunday reflect on the new ideas you gained during the past week. Enter them into a journal with comments on how you plan to use them. Brainstorm relationships among the ideas. Review the entries you made last week, three months ago, and six months ago.

Take time to deliberate, but
when the time for action has
arrived, stop thinking and go in.

—NAPOLEON BONAPARTE

Make better decisions.

Success comes from making sound decisions: College or job? Married or single? This person or that one? Repair or buy new? Rent or own? This job or that one? Now or later? You can make the best choices.

Yes, You Can!

༄

§ Recognize that you will never have perfect information for making important decisions. Set the goal of making *good* decisions with *sufficient* information within a *limited* time.

§ Define the problem to be solved. What exactly is the gap between where you are and where you want to be?

§ List as many options as you can to close this gap. Be creative; ask others for their suggestions. Don't jump on the first good-looking alternative, and don't stop until you run out of ideas.

§ Determine the criteria your final decision will satisfy. What "musts" will you insist upon, what "wants" will you hope for, and what is their relative importance?

§ Apply your criteria to all the options. Then select the one that meets all the must conditions and does the best job of achieving your most important wants.

§ Before you implement your decision, ask yourself what might go wrong with it. Prepare yourself to solve possible glitches down the road.

§ Get feedback. Can others find flaws in your thinking that could keep you from getting to where you want to be?

§ Act on your decision. Don't second-guess yourself, but if new information comes to light, be flexible and revise the decision.

§ When you're paralyzed, own up to the cause. Is it perfectionism, insecurity, aversion to risk, fear of failure, or hoping to be all things to all people?

Genius is the gold in the mine; talent is the miner who works and brings it out.

—LADY BLESSINGTON

Discover your hidden talents.

Most people fail to unleash most of their abilities during their lifetime. You have talents and potential skills that may never become known to you and shared with the world. Can you uncover your unique gifts?

Yes, You Can!

๛

๑ Try new things. Take on new assignments. Consider new career directions. Experiment with your aptitudes. Keep searching for your niche.

๑ Write this at the top of a sheet of paper: "Things I really enjoy doing." Carry this sheet around with you for a week, making entries as you think of them. At the end of the week, study the list and ask yourself how closely it corresponds to what you actually do. Any items on the list that are not now a part of your life and work may represent hidden talents.

๑ At the top of a second sheet of paper write: "Things I did well years ago but have stopped doing." Each entry on this sheet is a potential forgotten talent.

๑ At the top of a third sheet of paper write: "Things I do that people compliment me on or say I make look easy." These may be talents for which you want to find a larger outlet and more opportunity to apply.

๑ Ask people close to you these questions: "Do you think I'm making the best possible use of my abilities? Is there something you believe I have the ability to do that I'm not doing? Have I missed my calling?"

๑ What do you do apart from work? Which of your talents is evident in the groups you join, the volunteer work you do, and the hobbies you enjoy? Find ways to apply some of these talents more fully in your work and in your family life.

I used to think that anyone doing anything weird was weird. I suddenly realized that anyone doing anything weird wasn't weird at all, and it was the people saying they were weird that were weird.

—Paul McCartney

Increase your creativity.

Creativity is using your mind to change, revitalize, and reorder portions of your life. You're creative when you make something new based on what you perceive in the world. You're born with some creativity, but you can develop it much further.

Yes, You Can!
∞

- Think like a child. Play with ideas; ask "why not?" and "what-if?"; believe that there's always a better or a different way. Engage in new activities that have always fascinated you.

- Daydream about what you're working on. See fragments of it in your mind's eye. Move them around in your brain. Capture the new ideas popping into your head.

- Use "mind mapping" when you're planning a new speech, report, seminar, or project. Write the central idea in the middle of a sheet of paper. Draw a dozen or so lines emanating out from the central idea like rays from the sun. Over a period of days, brainstorm all the major ideas you might cover, positioning them on the ends of the rays. When your creativity is finally spent, cluster the many ideas into three to five main points. Focus on those.

- Don't fear mistakes. Creative people make them and profit by them.

- Associate with people who will prod you, question your assumptions, and help sharpen your ideas.

- Keep inspirational people by your side—those who encourage risk taking and thrive on change.

- Experience your innate creativity by doing something for the sheer joy of it without worrying about results.

- Become absorbed in the task at hand. Concentrate so intently on what you're doing that you begin to see clearly the many ways in which it can be improved.

God gave us memory that we might have roses in December.

—JAMES M. BARRIE

Improve your memory.

You can't remember the name of someone you met two minutes ago; you forget the combination to your safe; the digits of a private phone line escape you; last year's sales figures become a blur when you need to recall them. Can you do better at retaining important facts and figures?

Yes, You Can!
᪥

- § Exercise moderately, but regularly. You'll improve your memory by enhancing your strength and cardiovascular condition, lessening stress, and improving digestion and sleep.

- § Keep a diary for a month, recording your memory lapses. Do you tend to forget names, telephone numbers, appointments, facts, or something else? On which areas do you need to focus your memory improvement?

- § Look over material you need to memorize, then let some time pass before you review it again. Double the time before you look at it again. Keep doubling the time between reviews.

- § Do this to remember names: *listen* to the pronunciation of the name while looking intently at the person; repeat the *full* name; translate the name into a familiar object and juxtapose it on an unusual facial feature of the person; later, look back at people you've met and associate names with faces.

- § Remember lists of items by turning them into pictures that you connect together in your mind's eye.

- § Use the phonetic alphabet of consonants and consonant sounds to translate hard-to-remember numbers into easily recalled mental pictures. [1 = *t, d;* 2 = *n;* 3 = *m;* 4 = *r;* 5 = *l;* 6 = *ch, sh,* soft *g;* 7 = *k,* hard *g;* 8 = *f, v;* 9 = *b, p;* 0 = *s, z, cks.*] Thus, 57,443 becomes "locker room."

- § Use the time just before you go to sleep—preferably while relaxing in bed—to commit things to memory.

Not every woman in old slippers can manage to look like Cinderella.

—DON MARQUIS

Wear flattering clothes.

Your clothing presents an image that shouts volumes to others about your attitudes, your accessibility, and your ability. Even though the judgments people made about you will vary from person to person, to ensure that you make a good impression, there are certain sensible guidelines you can follow with confidence.

Yes, You Can!

&

§ Meet the expectations of people around you for your attire. Don't shock, disappoint, or embarrass them. Don't break the dress code where you are.

§ Wear what makes you feel comfortable. If you are at ease, you're likely to make others feel that way.

§ Dress according to the impression you want to give—formal/informal, intellectual/practical, staid/fun-loving, wealthy/poor, conservative/risk-taking, contemporary/old-fashioned.

§ Dress like people with whom you want to create rapport. Make them feel that you're one of the gang.

§ Wear what other people think you look good in. This requires that you keep close track of the compliments you get when you wear certain outfits, combinations, and colors.

§ In business settings, wear black or navy to build credibility. Gold, green, gray, or brown won't flatter most skin tones. Pale pastels can work; loud ones are gaudy. Light shades of blue, gray, and beige can look nice, but they may not be "power" colors.

§ Take care of your clothing. When signs of wear appear, relegate an item to casual settings. Avoid trendy colors and fashions that will become outdated a year later.

§ Buy the most expensive clothing you can afford from a clothier whose advice you trust.

To enter one's own self,
it is necessary to go armed
to the teeth.

—PAUL VALÉRY

See yourself as others do.

Success comes from your ability to influence and motivate others through your behavior. Can you find out what others think of your behavior?

Yes, You Can!

℘

$ Get feedback. Ask yourself how you think a particular person or group sees you. Make a list of the three most helpful and the three least helpful behaviors you believe they see. Ask them to indicate their agreement with your list, and maybe even to add a few items to the list.

$ Look at and listen to the feedback you already receive. Study the body language of other people when they're in your presence. Take note of their tone of voice; compare it to the tone they use with others.

$ Think back on the feedback you've received over the years— both the compliments and the criticism. What are the trends and themes in this feedback?

$ If someone is reluctant to comment openly on your behavior, bring up the name of a third person you both know. Ask, "What do you think [the other person] would say about my behavior?" Expect to hear what the *first* person really thinks.

$ Under the supervision of a licensed psychologist, take one of the many personality inventories, preference tests, or skill assessments that are available.

$ Videotape a presentation you make or a meeting you lead. Review it with someone knowledgeable and honest enough to give you helpful feedback.

$ When you're out and about, check your appearance in mirrors. Take a peek at what you show to the world.

$ Listen to yourself as you speak. Limit thinking and worrying about what you're going to say next and instead focus on your words and the way you say them.

Act Powerfully

The most savage controversies
are those about matters as to
which there is no good
evidence either way.

—BERTRAND RUSSELL

Win an argument.

Many people get trapped in debates they cannot win—not sure of what they're going to say, not anticipating what their adversary will say, failing to define their terms, and not even sure what the argument is all about. Can you avoid these snares?

Yes, You Can!

❧

- ❦ Pick your fights. Confront others only when you can predict at least a draw.

- ❦ Develop a reputation as someone who admits to being wrong when your errors are revealed to you. This encourages others to believe your assertions.

- ❦ Know your adversary. Prepare for likely tactics and plan to push suspected hot buttons to get your way.

- ❦ Know why you're arguing. Do you have a need to win, to work off your aggressions, or to establish a pecking order in the barnyard? Do your reasons make sense?

- ❦ Provide an alternative for anything you may be arguing against. Don't knock down the ideas of others without having something to put in their place.

- ❦ Let the other person speak first: your adversary will become a better listener, and you will gain clues to what it will take to convince him or her.

- ❦ Base your argument on facts. Use documented statistics. Quote respected people. Cite universal principles.

- ❦ Keep your cool while revealing a well-modulated sense of annoyance, even anger.

- ❦ Save sarcasm, incredulity, and caustic humor for your toughest and most uncooperative adversaries.

- ❦ Develop a win-win mentality. Aim to meet both your needs and those of the other person, rather than defending a one-sided and self-serving position. Never try to win by destroying an opponent. Attack issues, not people.

In business, you don't get what you deserve, you get what you negotiate.

—CHESTER L. KARRASS

Negotiate successfully.

In an ideal world everyone would get what they deserved. The world we *live* in is one of give and take. You can learn how to give the minimum away for the maximum return.

Yes, You Can!

༃

- ৡ Set a friendly, cooperative, trusting tone at the outset.

- ৡ Strive for a win-win outcome. Any resolution where you walk away with all the marbles sets the stage for future problems.

- ৡ Ask lots of questions and listen to the answers. Get to know the other person as well as you can. Knowledge of the other person's needs, expectations, preferences, peculiarities, aspirations, pressures, and strategies will tell you what you'll need to offer to reach an understanding.

- ৡ Find an agreement that meets your needs while meeting the other person's needs at the least cost to you.

- ৡ Know your "bottom line." Don't give any more than your maximum or accept any less than your minimum.

- ৡ Stay calm and rational during deliberations. As soon as either of you become emotional, call for a break.

- ৡ Don't appear anxious for a solution; don't make snap judgments when someone makes a new proposal.

- ৡ When you reach an impasse, do one of the following: take a recess; summarize your progress; restate the implications of not reaching an accord; suggest a new approach; talk about how you feel; give up something in trade.

- ৡ Ask these helpful questions: What else? What do you have in mind? What's your offer? Is there a possibility for more? What else do I need to know about this? What if I were to offer . . . ? Is the offer clear? What do you need? What will it take to get an agreement?

- ৡ Never go up or come down without getting something in return.

I shall tell you a great secret, my friend. Do not wait for the last judgment; it takes place every day.

—ALBERT CAMUS

Act ethically.

Illegal behavior violates the law. Unethical behavior violates a trust, a principle, or an accepted practice. Acting unethically means taking advantage of the kindness, weakness, or ignorance of others for your own personal gain. You can overcome the temptation to be unscrupulous.

Yes, You Can!

☙

- Ask yourself these two questions: What options do I have other than the unethical one? If I succumb to temptation, will I be able to look my spouse (friend, coworker, child, and so on) in the eye and say what I did?

- Recognize that unethical behavior will be observed by others, some of whom will lower their opinion of you.

- Don't be seduced into practicing situation ethics. Ethics are standards that don't change. They are unaltered by events. *Example:* You cannot justify committing a wrong because of a string of bad luck or in response to a host of inequities perpetrated against you. Hold dearly to your principles.

- Remember the pangs of conscience you felt the last time you gave in to temptation. Be assured that the agony will return if you compromise your values.

- Before you do something you'll regret, talk to people whose opinions you respect. Ask them for reasons why you should not carry through with your intent.

- Close your eyes and visualize the unethical action you are about to take. Make it grow very large (monstrously so), get very bright (even blinding), and make a screeching (almost deafening) sound. Now, shrink the size, kill the brightness, and snuff the sound by moving the picture away from you until it becomes a speck and disappears. Consider it gone!

- Read Ayn Rand's *The Fountainhead.* Could you have stood up as well as Howard Roark did?

When I'm getting ready to persuade a man, I spend one third of the time thinking about myself—what I'm going to say—and two thirds of the time thinking about him and what he is going to say.

—ABRAHAM LINCOLN

Sell your ideas persuasively.

If you want more success at winning cooperation from others and in getting them to go along with your suggestions, this list is for you. With the help of the tips below you can improve your ability to market your ideas.

Yes, You Can!

&

§ Store up credibility for when you need it by being known as someone who cares for others, who makes reasonable requests, and whose word can be trusted.

§ Know exactly what you are asking for. What new behavior do you expect? What are your precise expectations? What long-term implications should the other person understand before agreeing to comply?

§ Recognize *why* you are making this request. What's your ultimate goal? Will it in fact be achieved by the request you're about to make, or might you be asking for the wrong thing?

§ Be prepared to pay the price. What will this new behavior eventually cost in time, money, personal involvement, follow-through, negative reactions by others, altered results in a related area, the expected return of the favor, or another behavior in support of or in response to the person who cooperates with you?

§ Ask for it! Don't hint, wish, or wait for the other person to figure out what you want. Get to the point. Paint the exact picture you see of your need. And *believe* that you'll get a yes so that you can ask convincingly.

§ Be certain you're asking the right person—someone who can help; someone with the power to deliver.

§ Show benefits. Demonstrate to the other person in the most vivid language possible the value of fulfilling your request. Reveal the ways in which the action you're requesting will either remove pain from that person's life or introduce new pleasure into it.

A certain amount of opposition is of great help to a man. Kites rise against, not with, the wind.

—JOHN NEAL

Overcome objections to your ideas.

When you ask people to do something, expect a reason or two why they can't or don't want to do it. You can learn to overcome objections to your ideas, and possibly even turn reluctance into an advantage.

Yes, You Can!

&

- Know the people you sell to so well that you can build solutions to their predictable objections into your "sales pitch."

- State the objection you expect them to raise. Affirm that it's a valid concern. Then, while they look on as spectators of the objection—rather than owners of it—dismantle it, showing how your proposal eliminates it as a problem.

- When an unexpected objection comes up, listen to it. Be certain you understand it and can empathize with the other person's concern before proceeding to address it.

- Don't attack those who object to your ideas. Ask them to substantiate the assumptions behind their resistance.

- Restate each objection you hear to ensure you understand it. Repeating an objection back to its owner often weakens it.

- Don't argue, become angry, or get defensive. Remain calm, yet maintain visible enthusiasm for your idea.

- Test objections to be sure you know what you're up against. Ask this: "If I can prove that I'll take care of that, will you go along with my idea?" If the answer is yes, you know what you have to do to overcome the objection. If the answer is no, you haven't yet uncovered the real objection.

- Answer each objection with the facts that you believe will dismantle it. Demonstrate why your idea is not invalidated. Confirm with objectors that their concerns have been addressed. If you believe an objection *does* kill your proposal, ask for time to go back to the drawing board to reshape it.

- When objectors refuse to accept your solutions, ask them to provide their own. Many times they will!

I'm going to stop putting things off starting tomorrow.

—SAM LEVENSON

Stop procrastinating.

Although putting off an unpleasant task from time to time is not serious, chronic stalling is a problem. You waste time worrying about what you have to do, your mind magnifies beyond all reality the pain you will experience by doing it, and you risk letting down the people who are counting on you. You can get things done on time.

Yes, You Can!
✇

§ Spend the next week invoking the twenty-four-hour rule. Respond to each new stimulus—mail, requests, phone calls, and so on—within twenty-four hours.

§ When a new task looks overwhelming, start it immediately—even if you can only spend a few minutes on it.

§ Break every difficult task into manageable pieces. Work on one piece each day.

§ Stop thinking about how uncomfortable you think you'll feel while performing an undesirable task; start thinking about how good you'll feel when the job is done.

§ Reward yourself for making progress on a challenging project. Give yourself a bonus by doing something you really like.

§ Write a schedule for completing your work. Keep it in a highly visible place.

§ Make public commitments to starting and finishing scary tasks. It's easier to let yourself down than to embarrass yourself in front of others.

§ Recognize that you reduce your stress level every time you accomplish one of your "to dos."

§ Put this book down. Start working on the most nagging task in your backlog. Don't turn this page until you feel good about the progress you've made.

When you're through changing,
you're through.

—BRUCE BARTON

Accept change.

Three things in life are certain: death, taxes, and change. And of these three, most of us handle the first two better than the third. You can become more positive about coping with the change in your life and learn to use it to your advantage.

Yes, You Can!
☙

- Recognize that resistance to change comes from the fear of loss. Whenever the need to change troubles you, ask yourself what you're afraid of losing. Is it control? Prestige? Self-esteem? Closeness? Freedom? Comfort? Income? Identify the root of your resistance and take steps to overcome it.

- Accept the discomfort caused by ambiguity and uncertainty as a natural by-product of change.

- Identify the drawbacks of not changing. What will result if you fail to solve this problem, exploit this opportunity, or comply with this requirement? Isn't the status quo far more costly than transition?

- Identify the gain associated with changing. Don't allow your obstinacy to obscure the real advantages of moving from your present state to a new one.

- If the reasons for change are not clear to you, ask those who are initiating it. Don't make a snap judgment about its value. Give yourself a few days to become both emotionally and intellectually committed to it. Write down five advantages of the change before you allow yourself to dwell on its disadvantages.

- Take on the positive views of life that many people who are willing to change have in common. *Examples:* life is rewarding; there are important lessons to be learned from challenges; disruption is a natural element of an evolving world; and change presents opportunities to grow.

- Recall that the two symbols in the Chinese ideograph for *change* signify "threat" and "opportunity."

Many people's tombstones should read, "Died at 30. Buried at 60."

—NICHOLAS MURRAY BUTLER

Create a meaningful legacy.

A recent study of people over the age of ninety-five reported that one of their greatest regrets was their failure to leave behind something of worth to humanity. Even with limited financial resources, you can leave the world a better place.

Yes, You Can!

❧

- ◈ Raise positive children who want to make a valuable contribution to society. Teach them everything you know.

- ◈ Be a positive role model to the children in your life.

- ◈ Make whatever gift you can afford to a philanthropic foundation. Your contribution will enlarge its endowment, enabling your money to work for good for a long time.

- ◈ Make whatever gift you can afford to any organization whose goal is to educate youths in leading productive, healthy, and moral lives. Fund camperships for disadvantaged children.

- ◈ Find opportunities to work with young people. Volunteer at your school, church, or synagogue. Get involved with other organizations, such as the Scouts, that benefit the adults of tomorrow.

- ◈ Develop your teaching skills. Look for opportunities within your organization to train new employees so that they can advance their careers, feel better about themselves, and accomplish more for the customers of the organization.

- ◈ Will your vital organs to an organ bank. Tell your family about your decision.

- ◈ During your lifetime, work for the preservation of the environment. Produce less garbage and recycle what you can.

- ◈ Speak out against social ills, moral evils, and human suffering. Be a gadfly for good.

CHAPTER 3

COMMUNICATE EFFECTIVELY

If thou thinkest twice, before thou speakest once, thou wilt speak twice the better for it.

—WILLIAM PENN

Wisdom is the reward you get for a lifetime of listening when you'd have preferred to talk.

—DOUG LARSON

Listen better.

Someone in your life may need more of your attention, more of your concern, and more of your ears. You can understand this person better and make him or her feel better by being a good listener.

Yes, You Can!

ॐ

§ Set a personal goal for yourself of becoming a better listener. Accept nothing less than success.

§ Remain equally open to every idea you hear. Hold your fire. Don't stereotype the speaker, and don't make snap judgments on the value of what's being said until the speaker has finished.

§ Find personal value in hearing and being entertained by the stories of others.

§ Prepare to listen by thinking about the speaker in advance.

§ Shut up! Speak less. Bite your tongue. Say to yourself, I am going to empty this person of every emotion, thought, and opinion on this topic before I reveal mine.

§ Listen for content rather than judging, and therefore becoming distracted by, the speaker's delivery style.

§ Look at the speaker's body language and listen to the tone of voice to pick up meaning beyond the words being spoken.

§ Fight any visual, aural, or sensual distractions.

§ Give the speaker steady eye contact and get into an attentive body posture.

§ Focus on the speaker's message. Mentally summarize; weigh the evidence; ask clarifying questions.

§ When someone begins to speak, pick up a pencil. Make it a "listening stick" by squeezing it with your thumb on the eraser. Don't interrupt until the person stops talking. Then release the pencil and allow the other person to use it while you talk.

If all my talents and powers were to be taken from me by some inscrutable Providence, and I had my choice of keeping but one, I would unhesitatingly ask to be allowed to keep the Power of Speaking, for through it, I would quickly recover all the rest.

—DANIEL WEBSTER

Speak with impact.

Some speakers command attention. They sound convincing, authoritative, and credible. Their discourse has none of the self-effacing qualities that too many people allow to sap the energy from their ideas. Can you rid your conversation of power-robbing phrases?

Yes, You Can!
❧

§ Don't discount your ideas before you express them. ("You may not think much about this idea, but . . .")

§ Don't discount yourself before you give your opinion. ("While I'm not an expert on this topic . . .")

§ Don't qualify your message with wishy-washy modifiers. ("Sometimes, but not always, this is true.")

§ Don't seek permission to speak. ("I wonder if I might be allowed to say something.")

§ Don't rehash, repeat, and paraphrase unnecessarily. State your idea once, concisely, and directly.

§ Don't connect tag questions to the end of your statements. ("This is an important idea, don't you think?")

§ Don't demean or belittle your listeners. ("Let me put this in terms you can understand.")

§ Avoid clichés. You won't impress people by reminding them that you can lead a horse to water but you can't make it drink.

§ Use positive statements. Change "I don't mind helping you" to "I would enjoy helping you."

§ Avoid participial forms. Say, "I plan to do it," not "I am planning to do it."

§ Avoid the passive, impersonal voice. Replace "a decision was made" with "we decided."

§ Use the word *you* three times for every time you use the word *I.*

Suit the action to the word, the
word to the action.

—WILLIAM SHAKESPEARE

Send strong nonverbal messages.

As little as 10% of the impact of your spoken message is carried by the words you utter. As much as 40% is achieved by *vocals* (tone, inflection, emphasis, pitch, rhythm, volume, rate). More than 50% comes from your *body language* (eyes, face, hair, gestures, posture, cosmetics, accessories, clothing, actions, and use of space). Can you harness the 90%?

Yes, You Can!
❧

§ Study others' nonverbal messages. Note their impact.

§ Get feedback on your vocals and body language. Have someone observe you in a meeting. Record your voice. Videotape yourself making a presentation.

§ Look people in the eyes when you speak to them and when they speak to you.

§ Groom yourself carefully in the morning. Many people will judge your value by your looks.

§ Dress to meet expectations of important people. The look and quality of your attire should be slightly better than contemporaries. Wear what others have said you look good in when you need to influence them.

§ Correct your posture. Lift your collarbone one inch.

§ Never point a finger at anyone. Be careful of other potentially offputting gestures.

§ Give a firm (not vice-tight or noodle-soft) handshake.

§ Send positive messages with the settings in which you live and work. Is your desk messy? Is your car clean? What impressions do others get entering your home?

§ Nonverbals show how you feel inside and *determine* how you feel inside. Walk with your head up and you'll feel up. Wear your finest duds, you'll feel great. Get yourself excited.

The ability to speak is a shortcut to distinction. It puts a man in the limelight, raises him head and shoulders above the crowd, and the man who can speak acceptably is usually given credit for an ability all out of proportion to what he really possesses.

—LOWELL THOMAS

Speak eloquently.

A good speaker is not the one who remembers what to say, but rather says what will be remembered. This person is expressive, articulate, and well-spoken. You can learn such eloquence.

Yes, You Can!
℘

§ A well-timed, well-fitting quotation adds validity to your ideas and makes you look well-versed. Purchase a good book of quotations for your reference library.

§ Memorize one quote a day to use in your typical communication situations. Post a favorite "quote of the month" in your car, kitchen, or office.

§ Listen to the classic speeches of our time. *Examples:* Martin Luther King, Jr. ("I have a dream"), John F. Kennedy (Inaugural Address), and Franklin Delano Roosevelt ("Day of Infamy"). Note the rhetorical devices they used to rivet audiences.

§ Use repetition to grab your audience (e.g., Martin Luther King, Jr.'s use of "I have a dream").

§ Use antithesis to produce memorable effects (e.g., John F. Kennedy's "ask not what your country can do for you—ask what you can do for your country").

§ Use alliteration to get attention (e.g., Gerald Ford claiming "my record is one of progress, not platitudes; performance, not promises").

§ Use the rule of three. When ideas are strung together in a series of three, the impact almost always exceeds that of a string of two, four, or more. The second sentence in the introduction above would have been weakened if we added the word "fluent" to the series.

§ Use rhetorical questions to win the audience over. Start a seminar in the use of eloquence by saying, "Who among you is fully satisfied with your ability to stir others to action?"

Words have weight, sound and appearance; it is only by considering these that you can write a sentence that is good to look at and good to listen to.

—W. Somerset Maugham

Choose powerful words.

The well-chosen word gives your speech, your letter, and your manuscript the power to attract, mesmerize, and persuade. You can use words that get the best results.

Yes, You Can!

☞

§ Avoid euphemisms—words that make concepts more "socially correct" but weaker. Don't *perspire* when you should *sweat*.

§ Leave no doubt as to your intent. "Do it as soon as you can" may tell me I can wait until I'm good and ready.

§ Avoid the technical language of your profession, the slang of your social group, or the idioms of your home town with those who won't understand them.

§ Forget every worn-out phrase you ever learned. Don't remind us that "you can't tell a book by its cover."

§ Favor shorter words. Don't *inquire* about an opinion; *ask* for it. Don't *utilize* what you can *use*.

§ Increase the power of your suggestion with specific, colorful language. Your claim of *interest* won't carry the same weight as your *excitement* or *inspiration*.

§ Speak in the active voice. "My love for you is shown by . . ." isn't as strong as "I show my love for you by . . ."

§ Don't overuse a verb, noun, or adjective in the same letter or speech. *Example:* You can give *fast* a rest with *breakneck, snappy, swift, quick, speedy,* or *brisk*.

§ Use friendly contractions (e.g., "I'll" for "I will") in all but the most formal communications.

§ Overcome sexist language: Use the term "girl" only if you use "boy" in the same or next sentence. Avoid the generic "he" when you mean a man *or* woman. Find substitutes for "-man" and "-men" word endings (e.g., say "mail carrier" instead of "mailman"). If a woman has a professional title (e.g., "Dr."), use it.

A great many people think that polysyllables are a sign of intelligence.

—BARBARA WALTERS

Improve your vocabulary.

What if your carpenters showed up without any tools? They'd probably strike you as incompetent amateurs. In the same way you'll have a hard time projecting a polished, professional image with a deficient vocabulary. Your words are the plane, chisel, drill, level, and sandpaper you use to form your ideas. Can you shape them in just the way you need to get the impact you want?

Yes, You Can!
ॐ

§ Don't equate enhancing your vocabulary with learning those fourteen-letter words that challenged you on the SATs. Having a powerful vocabulary is using the right word to get the desired result. Long, unfamiliar words only confuse and frustrate receivers of your messages.

§ Read voraciously. Consume one book a week. Alternate those that you read for fun with those on the lists of "great books." Read newspapers and magazines daily.

§ Devour newspaper columns on word usage. Play the word games in newspapers and magazines. Become a fan of the crossword puzzle in *The New York Times.*

§ Read any of the books written by noted wordsmith William Safire.

§ Read *The Art of Plain Talk* by Rudolph Fleisch.

§ Keep an excellent dictionary and thesaurus in your personal library or on your word processor.

§ Play Scrabble or some of the newer word board games.

§ Learn one new word a day. Find an opportunity to use it the next day.

§ Exercise your vocabulary at every opportunity. Join a group where you'll be called upon to speak and write.

§ Listen to great speakers. Learn from their use of the "king's English."

The difference between the almost right word and the right word 'tis the difference between the lightning bug and the lightning.

—MARK TWAIN

Reduce communication errors.

English is a language in which it's easy to make mistakes in grammar, usage, pronunciation, and spelling. But you can make fewer errors.

Yes, You Can!
⊗

- Don't say, "I will try *and* do that." Try *to* do it.

- Don't say, "I *could* care less," when you *couldn't* care less.

- Don't say, "Between you and *I*." *Me* follows prepositions.

- Don't say, "*Can* I help you?" You mean *may*.

- Don't say, "I did *good* on the test," if you did *well*.

- Don't say, "He sent it to Jan and *myself*." *Me* is better.

- Don't claim that you would *of* when you would *have*.

- Don't say, "Each member must do *their* share." One correct way to avoid "his or her" here is to change the subject to "all members."

- Don't wait *on* a report when you should wait *for* it.

- Don't mistakenly feel *strongly* (or *badly*) about something you feel *strong* (or *bad*) about.

- Don't *lay* down when you mean to *lie* down.

- Don't use "irregardless"; "regardless" is correct.

- Use the preferred pronunciation of *harass, leisure, nuclear, realtor,* and *research.* Check your dictionary.

- Don't misspell *accommodate, benefited, canceled, changeable, commitment, consensus, disappoint, embarrass, etiquette, excel, existence, grateful, inadvertent, judgment, liaison, memento, minuscule, occasion, occurrence, omission, prerogative, perseverance, recommend, referred, resistance, seize, separate, supersede, threshold, tomorrow,* or *withhold.*

- Don't say you're *disinterested* in the results, when you're *uninterested* in them.

Make thyself a craftsman in speech, for thereby thou shalt gain the upper hand.

—ANCIENT EGYPTIAN TOMB INSCRIPTION

Improve your speaking voice.

Radio announcers are hired based on the quality of their speaking voices. Although many of them were born to utter resonant tones, most also employ strategies to improve the way they sound. You, too, can use these strategies.

Yes, You Can!
☙

§ If you want to overcome a speech impediment, first consider whether it is truly a hindrance to your effectiveness. (A professional speaker we know stutters without any loss in audience impact.) Get an expert assessment from a speech pathologist.

§ Listen to yourself on audiotape. What overall impression do you create with your voice? Do you vary your vocal impact to suit the message, or do you speak in a boring monotone or a repetitious singsong pattern? (Be prepared to detest the sound of your voice on tape.)

§ Repeat a sentence eight times, alternately voicing joy, fear, contentment, anger, embarrassment, sadness, surprise, and confusion. (Try, "You and I see that differently.") Have a listener give you feedback on the degree of the emotion you communicate.

§ Create contrast with your voice. Alternate between high and low, loud and soft, excited and reserved to highlight points you want your audience to remember.

§ Use silence and pauses in your speech the same way you use punctuation in written communication.

§ Articulate distinctly. Make a special effort to pronounce the final consonant in every word.

§ Practice speaking from deep in your diaphragm. Create vibration in your vocal cords. Don't talk through your nose.

§ Take care of your voice. A raw throat needs rest and humidification. Sip hot water or tea with honey—no lemon. Chew raisins.

Why don't th' feller who says, "I'm not a speechmaker," let it go at that instead o' givin' a demonstration?

—FRANK McKINNEY HUBBARD

Prepare compelling presentations.

Successful presenters know how to organize speeches that are fun to deliver and full of impact. You can learn their secrets.

Yes, You Can!
❧

❧ Base your speech on a clear purpose, stated in terms of how you plan to change—that's right, *change*—the audience. Recognize that nearly every presentation you make is a persuasive one, intended to get your audience to behave or think differently.

❧ Fit your approach to the mood, needs, knowledge, expectations, socioeconomics, experience, and self-image of your audience.

❧ Research the topic thoroughly; gather abundant evidence, statistics, and other supporting material.

❧ Brainstorm all the ideas you might present. Write these at random all over a large sheet of paper, representing a "core dump" of your thinking on this topic. Study the sheet and add ideas over several days. Finally, draw lines connecting like ideas, and select the *three to five* main points that you can best use to organize your material into a convincing argument.

❧ Create a set of notes containing trigger phrases—not sentences—that will enable you to deliver the speech with your eyes on the audience much of the time yet with constant awareness of where you are in the speech.

❧ Place vivid mental images of key points on attractive and easily seen visuals such as slides, charts, handouts, models, demonstrations, or write or draw on a board.

❧ Rehearse the presentation until you're comfortable with it.

❧ Arrange the room for maximum advantage and be sure to learn how to operate any equipment you plan to use.

*Speeches, like babies, are easy
to conceive but hard to deliver.*

—AUTHOR UNKNOWN

Deliver compelling presentations.

Give two people the same speech to deliver, and one will leave the audience more motivated to act. Can you consistently convince your audiences that your ideas are valuable to them?

Yes, You Can!
෴

- Open with enthusiasm. Deliver an attention-getting, interest-arousing, and rapport-building kickoff. And "tell 'em what you're gonna tell 'em" (reveal the speech's organization) early on.

- Add some humor by sharing personal stories, not by telling jokes or poking fun at your audience.

- Never open with an apology, such as "I'm not an expert on . . .," "If I'd had more time to prepare . . .," or "I'll be as brief as I can. . . ."

- Maintain eye contact with people in the audience.

- Avoid oral distractions, such as unnecessary utterances ("aah," "uhm," and "you know"), throat clearing, repetitive phrases, and incorrect use of language.

- Avoid physical distractions, such as poor posture, hair twirling, rattling your pocket change, swaying, leaning on the lectern, playing with a pen or marker, or doing anything repetitively.

- Inject vocal variety (changes in inflection, pitch, volume, emphasis, speed) into your delivery. Tie your conviction and confidence to your words.

- Control podium anxiety with the techniques offered on page 97.

- Stay within the allotted time; better yet, finish a little sooner than people expect.

- Close with a brief summary and a high-energy finish that motivates the audience to action.

The mind is a wonderful thing.
It starts to work the minute
you are born, and never stops
until you get up to speak
in public.

—JOHN MASON BROWN

Gain confidence as a speaker.

More than one opinion survey has shown that speaking before a group is our number one lifetime fear. But although it may afflict you much like a disease, you can overcome stage fright.

Yes, You Can!
∽

- Accept podium anxiety as a motivating force that even the most talented performers experience.

- Prepare so completely that your expert knowledge makes you feel invulnerable and unstoppable.

- Study your audience so thoroughly that you are sure you know how to push their "hot buttons."

- Rehearse your presentation from the very lectern in the very room where you'll deliver it.

- In the evening, before you retire, visualize success. See and hear yourself presenting with great confidence and enormous triumph. Enjoy a standing ovation.

- Involve your audience actively in your presentation from the beginning. Get them up on their feet; invite them to the front of the room to register opinions on a tote board; have them tell you the portions of your presentation they hope you'll emphasize. Share with your audience the responsibility to kick off a great speech.

- Use overhead transparencies or other audiovisuals to give the audience something to look at besides you.

- Expend a burst of energy by doing something strenuous just prior to stepping to the lectern. Take a brisk walk or climb a few flights of stairs.

- Use the squeeze technique to draw nervous energy out of your body through your arms. Fiercely clutch the sides of the lectern. Crush a flip chart marker in your fist. Pinch your fingertips together with your arms down at your side.

It usually takes me more than three weeks to prepare a good impromptu speech.

—MARK TWAIN

Learn to deliver impromptu presentations.

Speaking with the benefits of advance preparation, carefully planned notes, and eye-popping visual aids is one thing. Speaking without warning is quite another. Are you prepared to meet this communication challenge? Can you sound and look polished without warning?

Yes, You Can!

&

- Read everything you can get your hands on. To have the presence of mind to say something intelligent, you must have something intelligent to say. Keep up with current events and developments in your field.

- Keep a dozen or so favorite memorized quotations at hand. Use them to spice up unprepared remarks.

- When asked to speak, use the "rule of three." Think immediately of the angle you want to take on the topic, and put three main ideas in your head about that topic. These might reflect three challenges, three benefits, three methods, or three of anything else. You can also pose three questions you will answer in your talk (for example, what, where, and why).

- As you stand up, list your three main points. Then return to each one to elaborate. *Example:* An impromptu speech on buying shoes might begin, "When buying a pair of shoes, consider price, quality, and style. The price you pay . . ."

- Practice the rule of three from time to time to remain adept at it.

- *Know* that you look and sound good. Feel certain that you will succeed. Be buoyed by confidence, not defeated by doubt.

- Keep it short, and don't stray from the subject. It's better to leave them wanting more than wishing you had talked less.

- Reread and *practice* the preceding piece of advice.

If any man wishes to write in a clear style, let him first be clear in his thoughts.

—Johann Wolfgang von Goethe

Overcome writer's block.

Getting started may be the most difficult task when you sit down to write. You have all these ideas in your head, but you're just not sure how to introduce them or organize them. You're suffering from writer's block, but you can find a cure.

Yes, You Can!
❧

§ Ask yourself why you are writing this report, letter, or chapter. What do you want the reader to do or think about as a result of reading your work? As soon as you have the answer to this question, take a crack at an opening.

§ Skim paragraphs in a magazine, newspaper, or book for an inspiring literary device.

§ Set aside a half hour each day for writing as a means of reducing the overall intimidation factor.

§ Write first drafts freely and quickly with little concern for punctuation, spelling, neatness, or grammar.

§ Construct a storyboard. As ideas about your project come to you, jot them down on 3 × 5 cards and tack them on a wall. As you begin to see relationships among the cards, change their positions. As soon as the shape of your approach becomes clear, start writing.

§ Talk about your project with a friend or into a tape recorder. The more you talk, the more the ideas in your head will arrange themselves into a pattern in your mind's eye.

§ Place "who," "what," "where," "when," "why," and "how" down the left margin of a page, spaced about an inch apart. Write in the answers; then rearrange them into an outline you can work from.

§ Don't try to compose the introduction until the rest of the piece is written.

§ Write the conclusion *first;* then work on getting there.

In composing, as a general rule, run your pen through every other word you have written; you have no idea what vigor it will give your style.

—SYDNEY SMITH

Write persuasively.

We write letters, memos, and reports to sell ideas to others. But we aren't always as persuasive as we want to be. Can you do a better job of convincing others in writing?

Yes, You Can!
∝

⑤ In your document answer these questions for the reader: Why should I read this? What am I being asked to do? Why *should* I do it? What's in it for me?

⑤ Write with a "you" attitude. Put the reader in the message. Limit "I" statements.

⑤ Use the opening paragraph to get your foot in the door. Grab attention, pique interest, and build a psychological bond with your reader.

⑤ Support your arguments with evidence that is clear, credible, and compelling.

⑤ Write in the language of the reader.

⑤ Limit negative statements. Instead of telling readers what they can't do, tell them what they *can* do.

⑤ Use words that are sharp, crisp, colorful, honest, direct, and specific. Don't try to impress readers by using words they won't understand.

⑤ Go over your [first rough] draft [thoroughly] to [be sure to] eliminate [completely all of the] unnecessary words [and phrases] that [can] weaken your [entire] message.

⑤ State good news at the beginning of your message; withhold bad news until the end.

⑤ Close with a specific request. Let the reader know exactly what you want and how they can carry it out.

⑤ Read and use *The Elements of Style* by Strunk and White and *The Little English Handbook* by Corbett.

For a few brief days the orchards are white with blossoms. They soon turn to fruit, or else float away, useless and wasted, upon the gentle breeze. So will it be with present feelings. They must be deepened into decision, or be entirely dissipated by delay.

—THEODORE CUYLER

Express your feelings honestly.

As children we learned how to deal with our feelings. Perhaps the lesson you got was not to be honest about your reactions to what others do. As a result, you may have grown up walking on eggshells, afraid to speak your mind. You *can* be more free with your feelings.

Yes, You Can!

~

- If you learned to hide your feelings, you may realize that you've lost far more than you've gained over the years. If so, get mad enough about those losses to follow through on these ideas.

- Recognize that being assertive is not the same as being aggressive. Assertiveness is insisting that you be heard; aggressiveness is insisting that you get your way. Not everyone should get their way, but everyone—*including you*—should be heard.

- When you feel victimized, say so right away. Delaying the message only makes the eventual confrontation more difficult and increases your anger and frustration.

- Realize that every time you withhold a statement about your feelings, you drive a nail into the coffin of a relationship. Sublimated feelings never go away without scarring. You'll begin acting negatively toward this person for reasons that neither of you will readily understand.

- Never attribute to malice that which can be explained by incompetence—give others credit for stupidity. By stating your feelings you may point out behavior the other person is not aware of and would be willing to correct.

- Pick someone with whom you'll share an unexpressed feeling. Do it constructively, tactfully, and *honestly.*

- If you get a bad reaction to sharing your feelings, analyze the experience. Learn from the result, and vow to do better next time. Don't take it as proof that you should never again tell others how you feel.

CHAPTER 4

BUILD
RELATIONSHIPS

*The best time to make friends is before
you need them.*

—ETHEL BARRYMORE

Friends have all things in
common.

—PLATO

Develop immediate rapport.

Rapport is a common bond you create between yourself and others. This bond enables them to identify with you, encourages them to feel better about you, and prepares you to do a better job of influencing them. You can create immediate rapport with almost anyone.

Yes, You Can!

꙰

꙳ Greet people with a smile and a warm hello.

꙳ When you say hello and good-bye to people, use their names. Learn how to pronounce correctly the name they want to be called—ask to find out—and spell it correctly when you put it in writing.

꙳ Make a genuine inquiry about their family or about another topic important to them. Show interest in their interests.

꙳ Dress as they do.

꙳ Spend more time listening than talking. Continue to probe to get them to talk about what's on their mind.

꙳ Search for common passions. *Examples:* golf, fishing, child rearing, reading, antique collecting. When you find one, explore it thoroughly.

꙳ Ask people for advice on matters in which they consider themselves to be expert. Use it.

꙳ Listen to the person's tone of voice. Is it happy/sad, excited/lethargic, monotonic/varied, agitated/calm, loud/soft, high-pitched/low-pitched? Duplicate it to send a powerful, subconscious acknowledgment of empathy.

꙳ Observe the person's body language—especially eye contact, posture, and gestures. Match it as closely as you can, without being obvious, to send a powerful, subconscious acknowledgment of empathy.

The only way to have a friend
is to be one.

—RALPH WALDO EMERSON

Choose reliable friends.

Friends nurture us when we're in pain, console us when we grieve, and share in our delight when we rejoice. Do you choose friends who enrich your life in these ways or do you attract those who let you down, weigh you down, and take more than they give? You can do a better job of gaining friends.

Yes, You Can!

- Analyze your past failed relationships, answering these questions: What went wrong? Why? What role did you play in the failure? What will you do differently next time? What lessons did you learn about how to pick friends?

- Work gradually into friendships. Don't commit unconditional trust and undying allegiance without witnessing an impressive track record of reliability.

- Don't force friendships. Let rapport evolve naturally. "Let's be friends" is a nice sentiment, but it rarely serves as the inspiration for a long-term relationship.

- Have reliable friends by *being* a reliable friend. Enable the people in your life to count on you as much as you want to be able to count on them.

- Apply the knowledge that there are two kinds of people in the world—enemies and friends—and the difference between them is that enemies make you laugh while friends are willing to make you cry. Choose friends who will be honest in giving you feedback you may not get anywhere else.

- Insist that friendship be a two-way street. Be wary of acquaintances who get a lot more from you than you get from them. Surround yourself with givers.

- Pay the price in terms of time, energy, and commitment in order to have close friends.

There is the same difference in a person before and after he is in love as there is in an unlighted lamp and one that is burning. The lamp was there and it was a good lamp, but now it is shedding light too, and that is its real function.

—Vincent van Gogh

Build a loving relationship.

Like any organic system, a human relationship is subject to entropy—meaning that it is always in a state of decay. With a little effort you can counteract the tendency for your love relationship to fall apart.

Yes, You Can!
❧

- ৬ Create psychological intimacy. Share your innermost experiences and deepest feelings with the person you love. Talk daily about your impressions of the people and events you encounter; reveal your most important life goals; share your reactions to the triumphs and failures you experience.

- ৬ Maintain physical intimacy: hug and kiss in private; hold hands in public.

- ৬ Spend time each day discussing your "other lives"—your work, your families, your hobbies, and any other areas of life you may not always experience together.

- ৬ Make each other laugh—especially in a mature relationship where you may have forgotten the importance of being funny.

- ৬ Express love in ways that are important to your partner. Some need to *see* proof of love (for example, gifts or things you do); some need to *hear* proof of love (for example, saying "I love you" or giving compliments); some need to *feel* proof of love (for example, through hugs and kisses). Tell your partner which of these expressions you need.

- ৬ Each of you make a list of things the other can do to reinforce the feeling of being cared for. Do at least one thing on your lover's list every day.

- ৬ View the flaws you see in your lover as coal that hasn't yet turned into diamond. Don't plan or hope to change a thing. If you can't accept that "what you see is what you get," leave the relationship before it's too late.

No one can make you feel small
without your consent.

—ELEANOR ROOSEVELT

Protect yourself from abuse.

Some people become involved in relationships in which they feel emotionally victimized. No one should put up with abuse in any form. There are ways to gain freedom from mistreatment. You can make one of them work for you.

Yes, You Can!

∴

ś Refuse to enable chronic abusers by accepting their apologies. Instead say, "That apology may be real for you, but it's not real for me. The only thing real for me would be never to experience that again."

ś Refuse to enable chronic abusers by making excuses for their behavior to others.

ś Refuse to enable chronic abusers by protecting them from the consequences of their behavior. Allow them to feel whatever pain results from their actions.

ś Set an absolute limit on how much you will take, tell abusers what will happen if the behavior continues, and follow through on your promise.

ś Let go of an unrealistic dream for a relationship when others are unwilling or unable to reciprocate. Once the pain they cause becomes overwhelming, give them a final chance. Then cut your losses with remorse, but not guilt. Don't become a codependent who feels that the abuse is something *you* can control.

ś Pity your attackers. That's right: *pity* them. Once you are able to feel sorry for them for having such awful lives that they need to treat you badly, you can free yourself emotionally from the effects of their mistreatment. Pathetic figures can't push your buttons.

ś Memorize the Serenity Prayer: "God grant me the serenity to accept the things I cannot change; courage to change the things I can; and the wisdom to know the difference."

How many a dispute could have been deflated into a single paragraph if the disputants had dared to define their terms?

—ARISTOTLE

Disagree effectively.

Conflict is an inevitable by-product of relationships—both personal and professional. It's not a question of whether you'll fight with others, but how you'll fight. You can learn how to disagree more agreeably and successfully.

Yes, You Can!
crs

§ Think win-win, because you'll not win in the long run if the other person walks away humiliated. You'll pay somewhere down the line.

§ Focus on issues, not personalities, and remain calm. Name-calling and hurling accusations make a bad situation worse. The more upset you get, the less sense you make and the less credibility you have.

§ Listen to others' assertions before making yours. Once they've spoken their piece, they will be better listeners, and you will be armed with information to use when it's your turn to speak. You may even hear some valid points.

§ Ask lots of questions to learn *why* others believe what they are saying is true.

§ Limit your description of situations to what can be observed, as opposed to what you surmise or suspect. Deal in fact, not innuendo. When you assert your view, state *why* you believe what you believe.

§ Monitor and control your nonverbal communication. Don't tense up, point fingers, scowl, or get in the person's face. Maintain eye contact without glaring.

§ Fix the future, rather than rehash the past. Think long-term. Ask, "What will it take to keep this from happening again?"

§ Keep the focus on your comparative *needs*, not your opposing *positions*. Engage with the other person in a search for creative ways to meet both sets of needs and reach common ground.

Most of us would rather be ruined by praise than saved by criticism.

—NORMAN VINCENT PEALE

Accept criticism.

Only martyrs and masochists enjoy censure. The rest of us respond like children eating spinach—we know it's good for us, but we don't like it. Are there ways to be more open to criticism? Can you swallow your spinach?

Yes, You Can!

ॐ

§ Determine the criticizer's motive. If it is devious or hurtful, think—but don't say—this: "You have a problem that I can't help you with," and dismiss the criticism.

§ Agree that at least half of the reprimands given in this world are valid, and that you will probably get your share of them. Listen closely for the truth in what you hear—there may be some. You'll also learn a great deal about the person delivering the bad news.

§ View yourself as a work of art in progress. You won't be "finished" until you can't improve. Seek out opinions that can help turn you into a masterpiece.

§ Remember that pride cuts both ways. It has value in building your self-respect, but it's destructive when it causes you to be deaf and blind to feedback that might help you. Don't allow your pride to destroy you.

§ Object when criticism is directed at *you*, rather than at what you *do*. Tell scolders that you'll respond much better to a rejection of your behavior than an attack on your person.

§ Share your perception of the situation after the criticism has been delivered. Acknowledge the extent of your agreement with the comments, and point out your disagreement. Supply facts to correct inaccuracies, asserting your opinions firmly yet without annoyance.

§ Suggest a plan for corrective action that satisfies both of you. Learn whatever lesson this confrontation has taught you.

Speak when you are angry and
you'll make the best speech
you'll ever regret.

—LAWRENCE J. PETER

Control your anger.

Anger is a valid emotion—both to experience and to express. But you and the people around you are not served well by a steady diet of it. Can you learn to control your anger?

Yes, You Can!
⟡

  🕭 Get professional help if repeated rage is harming your life.

  🕭 Look at yourself in the mirror and say, "No other person makes you angry. *You* make you angry." Enter potentially anger-provoking situations refusing to be riled. Let your armor be the knowledge that your wrath won't serve your interests any better this time than it did the last time.

  🕭 Stop reacting below the neck, and start thinking above the neck. You are not destined to react with your gut and thereby lose emotional challenges. You *can* respond with your gray matter and win.

  🕭 Analyze the motives of those who push your emotional buttons. Recognize that others feel justified in behavior that looks irrational, childish, or punishing to you.

  🕭 Recognize that people who are mean, rude, or nasty to you are doing so not so much because they want to hurt you but because *they* are hurting. It takes considerable pain or fear to cause one person to lash out at another. Do you normally get angry with people who are hurt or fearful?

  🕭 Make an honest assessment of the typical results of your outbursts. Do you feel well served by them? If so, why are you reading this list? Resolve to stop shooting yourself in the foot.

  🕭 When you feel angry, stop talking. Inhale and exhale deeply, feeling anger leave your body with the spent air. Grab a pen and squeeze, feeling the anger escape through your fingers. Call for a short break and leave the room. When you're able to speak calmly, describe the anger you felt and move quickly to a solution that might meet the needs of the two of you.

I never expect to see a perfect
work from imperfect man.

—ALEXANDER HAMILTON

Accept others' imperfection.

"Beauty and the Beast" is a tale of accepting, and ultimately loving, the imperfections in others. Like Beauty in the fairy tale, you can accept other people as they are.

Yes, You Can!
⊗

§ Recognize that expecting perfection from other human beings is an act of arrogance. Stay off this high horse.

§ Recognize that expecting perfection means that other people must change for you. This gives others the message that they're not good enough; it is the ultimate act of rejection. Stop rejecting people, lest they start rejecting you.

§ Acknowledge that people who expect perfection are praise misers—in their eyes nothing is ever done well enough to warrant recognition. Force yourself to acknowledge the efforts of others. Begin today to say "thank you" in a sincere way to every deserving person in your life.

§ Refuse to relive the disappointment you set yourself up for each day when people fail to achieve the unattainable goals you set for them. Establish more realistic goals *with* them for their performance.

§ Look for special talents and skills in each person. Make a list and study it. Celebrate your good fortune to be living and working with such gifted people.

§ Think back over your upbringing to understand why and how your perfectionism was formed. Discovering its roots will help you to temper it.

§ On the left side of a sheet of paper record all the benefits of being a perfectionist. On the right side chronicle the pain and dysfunction—both yours and others'—associated with it. What does this analysis tell you about the value of continuing as you are?

*He who fights with monsters
might take care lest he thereby
become a monster.*

—Friedrich Wilhelm Nietzsche

Deflect aggressive people.

You were fortunate to get the last aisle seat on the plane for a cross-country flight. Just as you settle in, a tall imposing passenger confronts you and says, "My partner and I have separate seats but have certain matters to discuss. Your aisle seat is very important to us. You wouldn't mind moving into that center seat, *would* you?" Can you deflect aggressive people like this aisle assassin?

Yes, You Can!
&

- Avoid situations where you are likely to encounter physically hostile people. Shun dangerous neighborhoods, raucous bars, and excited crowds. When physical danger looms, run or get help immediately.

- *Prepare* for aggressive people. When you experience a loss at the hands of a pushy person, devise a plan for fending off similar aggression in the future.

- Repeat the person's request, embellished to your advantage. (In the airplane you might say, "You want me to give up this aisle seat that I worked so hard to get, so you and your friend can conduct business? I don't think so.") Make the request sound as outrageous as possible to the requester and to anyone else in hearing range.

- Thank others for their verbal acts of aggression as you deflect them. That's right: *thank* them. (The aisle assassin would have been totally closed off if at the end of the response just described you had added, "But thank you for asking.")

- Just say no. This may be tough for you to do, but it is the simplest and often the most effective response.

- When you say no, do so with a tone of finality and certainty. To make your no even more foolproof, have a smile on your face when you say it.

Words wound. But as a veteran
of twelve years in the United
States Senate, I happily attest
that they do not kill.

—LYNDON BAINES JOHNSON

Defuse angry people.

The pressure of work and the tension of life seem to be shortening everyone's fuse. Since there appears to be no reversal in the trend, expect to meet increasing numbers of irate people. Can you defuse their anger?

Yes, You Can!

༄

- Remain calm; don't let people push your buttons. You can't reason with them if *you* get angry. *Good ideas:* Count to ten; take a deep breath; see the outburst as a reflection on them, not you; tell yourself you'll succeed only by staying in your own head; think about something pleasant.

- Monitor the body language of antagonists. Remain alert for dilated pupils, flaring nostrils, rigid body posture, threatening movements, rapid breathing, and other warning signals. Move away, become conciliatory, or ask agitated people to talk about what they are feeling.

- Get the other person to sit down. We escalate on the balls of our feet, not on the cheeks of our seat.

- Listen, allow the person to vent, and don't interrupt. Show interest and concern in your face and eyes.

- After the venting is well underway, ask questions in a calm voice. Seek clarification and amplification, not justification.

- Empathize by saying, "I understand why you feel that way." Note that this is not the same as agreeing. It shows that you're listening and affirms that the person's feelings are legitimate—which they always are.

- Once you listen to everything the person has to say, offer or ask for a remedy that meets both your needs.

- When all else fails and the person continues to argue, ask, "What do you want me to do—what will make you happy?" Then either comply or say why you cannot do so.

If there were no bad people
there could be no good lawyers.

—CHARLES DICKENS

Handle difficult people.

A pundit once observed that there are two kinds of people: those who have ulcers and those who are carriers. If you have to live or work with carriers, you can learn to get the best out of them.

Yes, You Can!

∝

- ৩ Take a hard look at your behavior. Are you the match that ignites short fuses? Ask your close friends to help you answer this question. (If you don't have many close friends, you may already have the answer.)

- ৩ Let problem people express themselves without interruption. Listen to them and try to understand their feelings. Reflect carefully on their words before you respond.

- ৩ Ask for the change you want. Get to the point, but do so in a way that condemns the deed and not the doer. Recognize that performance—not people—is the problem. Attack and change behavior, not attitudes.

- ৩ Show people what you want by example. Let people see you doing the very things you are asking of them.

- ৩ Expect the best. Treat people as if they were already the way you want them to be. Let the self-fulfilling prophecy (the "Pygmalion effect") go to work for you.

- ৩ Allow difficult people to maintain their dignity and self-respect. Don't command, demean, or condemn them. Never cause them to lose face at your hands.

- ৩ Seek to understand people's motives so you can figure out what it might take to get them to change.

- ৩ Show people how it's in their best interest to adopt the behavior you request. Show them how they'll avoid pain or derive pleasure by going along with you.

- ৩ When progress is made, say "thank you."

Happiness is not so much in giving or sharing. We make a living by what we get, but we make a life by what we give.

—NORMAN MACEWAN

Give appreciated gifts.

The crowds in the shopping malls on December 26 are a good indication that not all gifts are prized by those who receive them. You can consistently please people with your presents.

Yes, You Can!

ॐ

ॐ Give unexpected gifts. At the birth of a baby, take a gift for the mother, father, or siblings. Remember events that aren't typically commemorated except by you. Send "just thinking of you" cards.

ॐ Carefully listen to and observe those to whom you give gifts. Discover what they truly enjoy receiving.

ॐ *Make* gifts. Handcrafted presents make a personal statement, especially if you don't typically create the gifts you give.

ॐ Give gifts wrapped in unusual packages or delivered in novel ways. An example would be a dozen roses given one day at a time.

ॐ Send thoughtfully written notes, either as gifts or along with your gifts. Write warm remembrances in books. Engrave keepsakes.

ॐ When you can't afford the real thing, give a miniature (for example, a toy model of a Porsche) with a personal note.

ॐ Pair a book with a related present (for example, a cookbook and gourmet ingredients).

ॐ Pick greeting cards carefully; pass on those that open with a negative statement (for example, "I may not tell you often enough how much I love you"). Write the person's name at the top of the message; underline phrases that are appropriate to your relationship; add a sentiment of your own.

ॐ Consider revealing planned surprises; the joy of anticipation may outweigh the pleasantness of a surprise.

ॐ Record a video- or audiotape for a loved one.

No one's head aches when he is comforting another.

—INDIAN PROVERB

Make others feel special.

You get the best results from people who feel good about themselves and good about you. Once you understand, accept, and *apply* this basic truth about human behavior, you can start immediately to build more meaningful relationships.

Yes, You Can!

៚

- ᎒ Listen. One of the highest compliments you can pay people is to show interest in their ideas and beliefs.

- ᎒ Apologize when someone feels hurt by something you've done. Admit to your errors and accept responsibility for your role in screwups.

- ᎒ Trust people by giving them more responsibility, self-determination, and freedom to act.

- ᎒ Show greater concern for people and their lives. Remember things about them—birthdays, anniversaries, and personal interests. Respond with empathy to their fears, concerns, and traumas.

- ᎒ Thank people who help you and praise them when they do a good job. Be generous with compliments.

- ᎒ Ask for things in a respectful way. "May I" and "please" need to find permanent homes in your speech.

- ᎒ Call people by name—the one acknowledgment unique to them. Use people's names whenever you greet them and say good-bye to them. And when you use a name, make certain it's the *right* name—the one the person wants you to use, pronounced accurately, and spelled correctly.

- ᎒ Keep people on your mind. Wonder how they're feeling about what's happening in their lives right now. The more you think about them, the more likely you are to empathize with them and act in ways that are considerate of them.

- ᎒ Ask people for their ideas and use those ideas.

Reprove thy friend privately,
commend him publicly.

—Solon

Allow others to save face.

One way the Japanese and the Western world view relationships differently involves the concept of saving face. The Japanese culture places a high value on protecting dignity and self-respect and on avoiding any possibility of embarrassing others. Can you do a better job of allowing others to save face?

Yes, You Can!
❧

§ Criticize only in private. And after doing so, give others positive strokes by saying something good about their performance, confirming your support of their efforts, expressing optimism for the future, or voicing your appreciation for their cooperation.

§ Criticize performances, not performers, saying "I" far more than "you."

§ Never point your finger at another person or make any other form of demeaning gesture.

§ Accept sincere apologies quickly, not allowing others to grovel.

§ Offer apologies quickly; admit to your errors easily.

§ Thank people when they retreat from a strongly held position, acknowledging how difficult it is to give in and how much you appreciate such a demonstration of goodwill.

§ Accept compliments and gifts gratefully and enthusiastically. Don't refuse or depreciate either one, thereby hurting the person who wants you to have it.

§ Talk *with* people, not *to* them. Guard against a condescending tone.

§ Stop demanding, commanding, or condemning. Live by the Golden Rule.

§ Look for ways to *serve* people.

Anger ventilated often hurries toward forgiveness; anger concealed often hardens into revenge.

—EDWARD ROBERT BULWER-LYTTON

Express anger productively.

Most of the time you will want to control your anger, but on occasion it may be best for all concerned to vent it. Sometimes the importance of your feelings won't be recognized in a more dispassionate discussion. You need not fear becoming angry. You can learn to handle it well.

Yes, You Can!
❧

- Save your anger for worthy causes. On a sheet of paper write down ten behaviors by others that anger you. Resolve to scratch five of them from the list in one of two ways: (1) recognize that your anger about this behavior accomplishes no good, or (2) take some positive action to change the behavior that upsets you.

- *Anticipate* situations in which you're likely to explode. Plan an expression of anger that communicates your indignation clearly without making you look out of control or irrational.

- Never seek to punish with your anger, and never allow it to turn into fury, frenzy, or hysteria. Use your anger instead to demonstrate frustration, irritation, and outrage.

- Stay at least five feet away from those to whom you are expressing anger. Both of you should be either standing or sitting; sitting is the preferable position.

- Make absolutely no physical threats.

- Do not engage in name-calling; do not say anything you will regret later (for example, "Get out of this house!"); do not use profanity; do not threaten to do something that you will not have the desire to do once you calm down.

- Start your complaint with the word *I*. Utter at least five sentences before using the word *you*. Discuss your *feelings* thoroughly. Accept responsibility for your anger before you describe the behavior that you have allowed to provoke you.

Take away love and our earth
is a tomb.

—ROBERT BROWNING

Cope with a breakup.

As the song goes, "Breaking up is hard to do." One of the most difficult periods in anyone's life follows the ending of a romantic relationship. But as hard as it may be, you can find ways to speed your recovery and get on with your life.

Yes, You Can!

☙

- ❧ Denial helps you to survive the initial shock (for example, "She'll return to me when she comes to her senses"). But don't remain in denial once the reality is clear.

- ❧ Don't allow anger to consume you. Your indignation will prevent you from acting intelligently and in a way that benefits your long-term best interest.

- ❧ If you feel guilty about something you did that may have precipitated the split, remember that both people are equally responsible for the health of a relationship. If you did something really bad, vow never to do it again in the future.

- ❧ Before you reach out in an attempt to patch things up between the two of you, be certain that both of you share a genuine commitment to making things different (better) this time.

- ❧ Expect to experience depression, which can be either a sign that you're starting to accept reality or a possible indication that you need professional help. Protect yourself by remaining isolated for a while from potential new relationships. One day you'll be ready to commit the old relationship to memory and prepared to follow a new energy in yourself.

- ❧ It may help to mark the end of the relationship with a private burial. Collect items that symbolize the relationship (for example, letters, photos, gifts) and bury them in your backyard as you speak whatever words will affirm that you are releasing this person from your life. Allow your feelings of anger, sorrow, or relief to flow.

CHAPTER 5

MOTIVATE & OTHERS

It is not the martinets that make an army work; it's the morale that the leaders put into the men that makes an army work.

—HARRY S TRUMAN

If anything goes bad, I did it.
If anything goes semi-good,
then we did it.
If anything goes real good,
then you did it.
That's all it takes to get people
to win football games.

—PAUL "BEAR" BRYANT

Gain respect as a leader.

It's one thing to be given the mantle of leadership; it's another to have those whom you supervise feel you deserve it. Follow the examples of the great leaders of our time and you can increase the respect you receive as a leader.

Yes, You Can!
℘

- Leaders *have vision.* They dream. Find out where you want to go, write it down, and get excited about it. Put something in your plan to excite the people around you, and then share the vision with them. Did Martin Luther King, Jr., do any less?

- Leaders *listen.* Learn the desires, aspirations, worries, and frustrations of your people. Find out what ideas they have for achieving your vision. Did Mahatma Gandhi do any less?

- Leaders *earn trust.* Be honest with people. Have your word be the most valuable thing you own. Did General Norman Schwarzkopf do any less?

- Leaders *uplift others.* Praise and reward those who perform well for you. Give them a piece of the pie. Did Sam Walton do any less?

- Leaders *maintain humility.* Give more credit to your people than they expect; accept more blame than you deserve. Don't get seduced by your own press clippings. Did Paul "Bear" Bryant do any less?

- Leaders *have fun.* Supervision isn't a penance. Drop your guard. Laugh at yourself. Create an atmosphere where smiles generate all the light needed to do the work. Did John F. Kennedy do any less?

- Leaders *serve.* Be more concerned about the welfare of your people than you are about yourself. Ask, "What did I do for my people today? How did I support their efforts? How did I motivate them? Did I give them what they need in order to give me what I want?" Did Moses do any less?

If you can dream it,
you can do it.

—WALT DISNEY

Create an inspiring vision.

As leader you are in charge of the big picture. Your people depend on you to articulate the values, beliefs, and mission that will drive the organization. You can meet their expectations and create a vision that will inspire them.

Yes, You Can!

❧

- Reserve time to dream. Disconnect from the fire-fighting pressure of work. Take exotic vacations; enjoy escape weekends; plan a few "mental health" days each year.

- Use time away from your regular routine to fantasize about tomorrow. Set new goals; dream up new products and services; ask what-if and why-not questions; search for new connections between old ideas.

- Your vision probably needs to be consistent with a larger vision—perhaps that of your boss, your division, or your company. Study their creeds, values, and beliefs for guidance and inspiration in forming yours.

- Put your vision down on paper. First address your *leadership role:* What changes do you foresee in that role? What plans do you have for bringing changes about?

- Form the larger vision of your company, your plant, your department, your store, or your team—depending on the level of your responsibility. Include value statements about your *people* (for example, rewards, recognition, development, diversity); your *organization* (for example, structure, decision-making authority, teamwork); your *business* (for example, satisfying customers, ethical standards, entrepreneurial spirit, long-term thinking); and your *environment* (for example, health, safety, environmental responsibility, role in the community).

- Share your vision with those who will join with you in attaining it. Better yet, let them help you create it.

The country is full of good
coaches. What it takes to win is
a bunch of interested players.

—DON CORYELL

Hire top performers.

What is the best way to deal with problem performers? Don't hire them in the first place! Both poor and superb workers were probably already that way when you chose them, so why not make the right choice in the first place? You can do it.

Yes, You Can!
☙

- You get what you pay for. Don't expect to attract headliners with understudy wages.

- Know what you're looking for. Make a list of the twenty most important qualities you need in the next person to fill the job. One of the behaviors that should be on every list for every job is that the person must be a team player. Organizations where people don't pull together fall apart.

- When you conduct interviews, use your list of desired qualities to frame each interview question.

- The best predictor of future performance is past performance. Learn what the candidate has accomplished *recently*. Pay less attention to experience and education. Find out if the person can do the job.

- Provide interviewees with a written list of your job performance expectations for the position. Discuss and assess the readiness of each candidate to fulfill those expectations.

- If the selection decision is to be made by committee, delay rating, ranking, or voting on candidates until their strengths, weaknesses, and any unanswered questions regarding each one are thoroughly examined.

- William Wrigley once said, "When two men in business always agree, one of them is not needed." If you're hiring an assistant, seek someone who thinks differently than you do. Favor candidates who are strong where you're weak and weak where you're strong.

Before you build a better
mousetrap, it helps to know if
there are any mice out there.

—MORTIMER B. ZUCKERMAN

Learn the needs of your followers.

How do you motivate employees? Put them into jobs where they can meet needs that are important to them while they do work that is important to you. Before you can help them meet those needs, you have to learn what those needs are. Can you find out what drives your workers?

Yes, You Can!

- Manage by wandering around. Spend time talking with employees. What desires do their words reveal? With what tone of voice do they discuss their work?

- Observe them doing their jobs. What desires do their actions reveal? What turns them on and off?

- Try them out on different tasks. Where do they shine, and where do they languish?

- Ask them what they like and don't like about the work they do now, and ask them to describe their ideal job.

- Convene an employee focus group to brainstorm ways in which work can become more motivating.

- Don't assume that you can stereotype employees or that all have pretty much the same needs. Acknowledge their individuality and uniqueness.

- Don't assume that what is important to you is also important to them. They may be more different from you than you think.

- Don't assume that they are interested only in the material benefits of work. *Do* assume that recognition, challenge, achievement, autonomy, personal growth, creativity, and meaningful work are just as important to them as they are to you.

- Administer a survey of employee attitudes about work.

- Conduct exit interviews. When employees leave voluntarily, find out what you might have done to keep them. Use what you learn to motivate existing staff.

He who knows, yet thinks that he does not know, has great wisdom. He who does not know and thinks he knows is diseased.

—LAO-TZU

Find out how followers see you.

The modern management mandate is to lead by example. One of the surest ways to get the loyalty, hard work, punctuality, creativity, initiative, thoroughness, dependability, and service you want from workers is to have them see these very same qualities in you. Do they? You can find out what kind of role model you are for your employees.

Yes, You Can!
ॐ

§ Watch for the nonverbal cues employees send your way. Do they speak in respectful tones? Do they seek your counsel? Are they relaxed in your presence?

§ Observe employee behavior. Do your workers willingly, and even happily, comply with your requests?

§ Ask employees to complete an opinion survey about the work environment and your leadership style.

§ Ask trusted colleagues what they hear from your employees about your leadership style. Probe for specifics. Ask for their suggestions on what employees want to see more of in your behavior.

§ Ask employees to fashion a list of twenty numbered leadership behaviors they need from you. Give each employee a bag of three lemons and three oranges. Ask for numbers on the fruit corresponding to behaviors on the list that reflect your best opportunities for improvement (lemons) and your greatest leadership strengths (oranges).

§ Videotape yourself running a meeting or conducting business in your office on a given day.

§ Ask your company to get "360-degree" feedback on you. This involves administering a leadership survey to your superiors, peers, and subordinates. The results are analyzed and returned to you by a consultant who then explains the implications of the data and helps you develop strategies to respond to it.

For if the trumpet give an uncertain sound, who shall prepare himself to the battle?

—1 CORINTHIANS 14:8

State your expectations clearly.

Many people work for "puzzles" who send mixed signals, give unclear direction, and fail to reveal their personal needs for employee performance. Many management experts claim that unstated expectations is the number one cause of poor performance by workers. You can avoid communication breakdown by being a leader who is clear about your expectations.

Yes, You Can!

❧

- ⑤ Aim to write twenty to thirty-five expectations in the form of a list. Any fewer and you may be missing important requirements. More and you may be guilty of micromanagement.

- ⑤ Begin each expectation with a verb, such as: *listen, speak, tell, avoid, use, learn, treat, perform, arrive, fix, keep, dress, maintain, suggest, deliver, pitch in.*

- ⑤ Make the expectations so specific that there is no room for doubt or unintended interpretation. *Example:* "Tell me whenever you disagree with one of my actions."

- ⑤ Cover each of these categories: communicating and reporting to you; dealing with your boss; relating to coworkers (for example, teamwork); supervising subordinates; treating customers; quality and quantity of work; work and personal habits.

- ⑤ When making the list, consult: the job description, previous performance appraisals, your impressions about how the job is being done, your boss, your colleagues, and your customers.

- ⑤ Go over your list with your boss, your colleagues, and possibly your human resources office before presenting it to employees. Be certain your expectations are clear, realistic, consistent, fair, and legal, as well as appropriate and necessary for quality output.

- ⑤ Consider having employees, rather than you, draft a list of your expectations of them. You can then refine the list and emerge with a final list that has their full commitment.

The buck stops here.

—HARRY S TRUMAN

Hold others accountable.

Many employees can be counted on to give their best without close supervision. Others need to be held answerable for their performance. You can hold *all* employees accountable.

Yes, You Can!
⚭

꙼ Put performance expectations in writing using the method explained on page 153. This list forms the basis for establishing accountability by serving notice of your precise requirements. Get a powerful commitment to the performance requirements by enlisting employees in their development.

꙼ Conduct periodic formal performance reviews. The more often you conduct them, and the more you base the reviews on written performance expectations, the greater employee accountability will be.

꙼ Invoke penalties, in the form of criticism or discipline when employees fail to take expectations seriously and dispense rewards when they embrace expectations and accomplish them.

꙼ Once an employee's behavior begins to become a problem, create a paper trail. Keep a private log of your concerns and a record of your efforts to correct the situation. After two or three oral reprimands, make each succeeding warning in writing, giving a copy to the employee and putting another copy in his or her personnel file. (Check this procedure with your human resources office before implementing it.)

꙼ Once you predict the possibility of having to formally discipline or fire a nonperforming employee, consult with your boss to make certain that he or she will stand behind your decision.

꙼ Show new employees by the way you treat others that you will hold them strictly accountable for their performance.

꙼ Demonstrate through your leadership behavior a low tolerance for mediocrity.

The deepest principle of
human nature is the desire to
be appreciated.

—WILLIAM JAMES

Give praise.

Many employees report working for praise misers—managers who haven't mastered the art of saying "thank you." Your employees need never feel unappreciated. You can learn how to motivate them through praise.

Yes, You Can!

❧

- The first step in becoming freer with praise is to recognize which of the following traits may be sealing your lips: having had an impersonal upbringing; expecting the best; holding employees to unrealistic standards; not taking the time; favoring the stick over the carrot; mistaking praise for a *reward* rather than seeing it as a *motivator.*

- Plan in advance to take advantage of the opportunities to praise employees for what will likely be outstanding outcomes or exceptional effort. Anticipate the victories they're likely to have. Prepare to celebrate them.

- Praise the deed rather than the doer. Point out specifically what people have done to earn your appreciation. Let them be pumped up by their work, not by you.

- Don't leave out any deserving employees when you praise. Acknowledge the contributions of "blockers" who clear the way for your leading "ground gainers."

- Praise sincerely. Have a smile in your heart and in your voice. Don't applaud employees only when you're in a good mood, don't pass out compliments like free samples, and don't make your praise sickeningly sweet or overly effusive.

- Praise publicly only when the recipient won't be embarrassed and when others aren't likely to react with resentment.

- Never negate praise. *Example:* Don't follow an acknowledgment of success with "I wish you would do it that way *all* the time."

No amount of pay ever made a
good soldier, a good teacher, a
good artist, or a good workman.

—JOHN RUSKIN

Motivate inexpensively.

Does money motivate people to work harder? Answer this question for yourself by picturing in your mind the hardest-working people you know and judging whether they perform as they do because of the money they make. Whatever your conclusion, the more important question may be: Can you motivate without spending a lot of money?

Yes, You Can!

- Write personal notes of appreciation to every member of a team at the completion of an important project.

- Publish an "Accomplishments of the Year" booklet describing victories and picturing the victors.

- Give plum assignments to hard workers.

- Take time to counsel employees on their professional development and on their career direction.

- Hand out tickets to sporting and cultural events.

- Buy copies of the latest business best-sellers for your team.

- Have lunch or take a break with a group of employees you don't often get to see.

- Find opportunities to give your employees credit, both orally and in writing. Get stories about them published in the company newsletter or in professional publications.

- Appear at initial meetings of focus groups, quality circles, and task forces to express your appreciation.

- Manage by wandering around. Show an interest in what employees are doing and thank them on the spot.

- Send employees to skill-building seminars.

- Let employees represent you at important meetings.

- *Best idea:* Ask employees how you can best show your appreciation, and give them what they want.

Do not use a hatchet to remove
a fly from your friend's
forehead.

—Chinese proverb

Criticize constructively.

Is *constructive criticism* a contradiction in terms? No! Criticism can elevate rather than annihilate, build up rather than tear down, and enhance rather than diminish. Can you give criticism that minimizes defensiveness in others and encourages them to improve their performance?

Yes, You Can!
❧

❧ Criticize in private. Criticize in private. Criticize in . . .

❧ You may want to find out first whether the person *wants* feedback. Ask, "Would you like a second opinion?" or "Do you want to know how I feel about that?"

❧ Before you open your mouth, examine your heart. Don't believe you can help—the goal of constructive criticism—while you feel angry, insulted, or wronged.

❧ Condemn the deed, not the doer. Separate the sin from the sinner. Say what you see. Focus on what happened rather than on what the person did. Avoid the word *you.*

❧ Say what's wrong with the behavior. Point to a specific negative impact on the organization, the team, the person, or you.

❧ Ask the person to explain what happened. There may be a good reason for his or her behavior. Find out.

❧ Paint a clear picture of what you expect in the future; suggest what corrective action is needed to get there. *Better idea:* Let the other person suggest the remedy. Ask, "What will it take to keep this from happening again?"

❧ Insist that the person make a commitment to a plan for improvement. Pledge your support.

❧ Thank the person for cooperating, express your optimism about the future, or praise a positive aspect of his or her performance.

❧ Don't stick around long enough to change the subject to something that will weaken the impact of the criticism.

Eighty percent of American managers cannot answer with any measure of confidence these seemingly simple questions: What is my job? What in it really counts? How well am I doing?

—W. EDWARDS DEMING

Evaluate performance effectively.

The annual performance review can be one of the most frustrating duties managers fulfill as well as one of the most anxiety-laden events that employees face. But it doesn't have to be that way. You can use reviews to improve employee performance, and employees can look forward to them as opportunities to receive valuable coaching.

Yes, You Can!
&

- Show the performance review form to job candidates during the employment interview and during orientation so they'll know what will be expected of them.

- Provide feedback throughout the year so that the content of the review does not come as a surprise. Don't save up criticism or praise for formal sessions. Increase the frequency of employee reviews to two, three, or even four times a year.

- Alter your role in the review from that of judge to coach. Get training on how to do this.

- Have the employee perform a self-assessment and talk as much as you do. Listen and ask questions.

- Rid your forms of rating numbers and labels (for example, "commendable"). Employees fixate on them and lose sight of making a commitment to improving performance.

- Replace performance adjectives (for example, "dependable") with statements about your specific expectations of the employee you are reviewing (for example, "Respond to requests for credit verification within twenty-four hours").

- Make sure that at least half your form is devoted to planning a course of action to improve performance.

- Give employees the opportunity to provide feedback on how well you are supervising them.

- Hold a follow-up meeting one month later to discuss performance progress.

Lord, make me an instrument
of thy peace. Where there is
hatred let me sow love. Where
there is injury pardon.

—ST. FRANCIS OF ASSISI

Resolve conflict among others.

When people around you react to stress or competition by going at each other's throats, you need the wisdom of Solomon. The job of referee isn't easy, but you can do it.

Yes, You Can!
☙

- Establish unequivocal office policies so as to minimize conflict. Be firm in your requirements regarding job performance, employee rights, ethics, treatment of customers, cooperation, dress, weapons, drugs, alcohol, and other concerns that your personnel officer or lawyer agrees are legitimate.

- Whenever you speak separately to conflicting parties, reserve the right to bring anything discussed to the attention of the other person if you decide that's best.

- When you invite conflicting parties to your office, set as ground rules that conversation will be controlled, civil, and free from accusations.

- Don't take sides; the antagonists need to have confidence in you and trust that you will remain impartial. Your role should be that of facilitator, not judge.

- Get the facts out. Let one person speak first without interruption. Have the second one paraphrase, to the first person's satisfaction, what the first person has said. Next hear the second person's side of the story in the same way. Continue until the parties either discover their communication breakdown or agree on what the conflict is all about.

- Ask for a resolution that all three of you can live with. If you like what you hear, go with it. If not, impose or negotiate a settlement of your own.

- Provide the opportunity for one party to save face should he or she be perceived as the loser. Show that person how important his or her cooperation is to you.

- Monitor the success of the resolution; react as necessary.

Few will have the greatness to bend history itself; but each of us can work to change a small portion of events, and in the total of all those acts will be written the history of this generation.

—ROBERT F. KENNEDY

Make change happen.

The "future shock" once predicted by author Alvin Toffler is here. Those who prosper in our inconstant world accept change as a positive force and can persuade others to do the same. Those fearful of change or unable to rally others in new directions will be steamrollered with the volatility of modern organizations. You can get others to go along with useful change with a minimum of resistance.

Yes, You Can!
❧

❧ Prepare for resistance. People fear change because they expect to lose something they value and because they have so often been victims of poorly administered change. Anticipate the exact concerns and objections you're likely to hear.

❧ Don't believe that resisters are being foolish or obstinate. Put yourself in their shoes to understand their fears. Then you'll be in a much better position to reassure them.

❧ Whenever possible, involve employees in deciding on and planning for the change.

❧ Explain the change fully. Give a rationale for it, the roles employees will play in it, and its implications. Emphasize the benefits to employees and to the company.

❧ Provide venting forums. Listen without comment. Acknowledge concerns; don't criticize or belittle them. Tell employees how you'll address their objections.

❧ Demonstrate management's commitment to the change. Do more than your share of work and accept more than your share of the sacrifices needed to implement the change.

❧ Make those organizational adjustments and resource reallocations needed to accommodate the change.

❧ Train, coach, counsel, and reward employees throughout the implementation phase. Be there for them.

The greatest good we can do
for others is not to share our
riches but to reveal theirs.

—AUTHOR UNKNOWN

Increase the self-esteem of others.

Some of your best performers may be limiting their effectiveness by not realizing just how good they are. You can pump up those who hold themselves back because of a negative self-concept.

Yes, You Can!

❧

- Help them set ambitious and specific goals for their professional development. See that they get started implementing those goals. It's difficult for people to maintain a low opinion of themselves while making progress on professional development goals.

- Don't allow them to ignore or dismiss their success. Reveal their victories to them by documenting successes on performance appraisals and in written commendations.

- Thank them personally whenever they achieve something important.

- Whenever any superior, peer, or customer compliments your subordinates to you, tell your employees what was said.

- Encourage higher-ups to take notice of your employees and to wander around on occasion to acknowledge them.

- Show people how their work helps others, and they'll feel better about it and about themselves. Reassign them to jobs that are obviously beneficial to others.

- Arrange for your subordinates to work with other positive, self-confident people whose attitude may rub off on them.

- Ask for employees' help and suggestions; use as many of their ideas as you can.

- Pump them up with opportunities to grow through training, education, and one-on-one coaching with you.

- Entrust them with increasing levels of responsibility. Give them greater challenges to meet.

Few things help an individual more than to place responsibility on him, and to let him know that you trust him.

—Booker T. Washington

Delegate to empower others.

Do you have more work than you can handle? Do you hesitate to take vacations fearing what will happen while you're gone? Do you have employees whose talents are not being fully tapped? You can relieve your burden and empower your employees by giving them increased responsibility.

Yes, You Can!
☙

- ֍ Understand why you don't delegate. If you manage close to the vest and are afraid to lose control, recognize that delegation increases your control by enabling you to *do* less and *manage* more. If you lack trust in your employees, note how the steps below increase the odds of employee success and give you total recourse in cases of failure.

- ֍ Inventory employee talents. What do they do well? What do they like to do? Where do they shine for you?

- ֍ Match the talent inventory to your responsibilities. Who has the ability, interest, and time to step in?

- ֍ Plan for the delegation of tasks. Who needs to know before you reassign work? Your boss? Peers? Customers? Other employees? What accommodations need to be made? What possible negative fallout or risk needs to be minimized? How?

- ֍ Talk with the chosen employee. State your expectations clearly. Explain the benefits of the assignment. Express your optimism that he or she will be successful.

- ֍ Support the delegation of tasks. Provide training, coaching, information, and the resources the employee will need. Praise both effort and accomplishments. Give the employee the authority needed to make decisions necessary to perform the task.

- ֍ Evaluate the results. Hold monthly reviews until you decide to rescind the assignment, revise it, or make it a permanent part of the employee's job duties.

Had God sent the Israelites a committee instead of Moses, they would still be in Egypt.

—AUTHOR UNKNOWN

Lead productive meetings.

Meetings can gobble up major time at work. They are also one of the most valuable communication tools at your disposal. When used correctly, meetings generate synergy and focus the energies of many on a unified goal. Can you lead productive meetings?

Yes, You Can!

൭

- ✤ Never meet without a written agenda specifying the date of the meeting, starting and ending times, the location, goals to accomplish, points to discuss, who should attend, and any preliminary work expected of participants.

- ✤ Use the first meeting to discuss what you expect from the members and what they expect from you. Agree on a mutual performance contract.

- ✤ Stick to the agenda. Keep social chitchat and digressions to a minimum.

- ✤ Listen to what people have to say, and influence participants to do the same. When someone expresses an important idea, don't let it go without a response.

- ✤ Carry a big stick. Step in to resolve disagreements; don't allow personal agendas to interfere.

- ✤ Study the nonverbal cues of group members for signs of confusion, boredom, or alienation.

- ✤ Don't allow decisions to be made without challenging the validity of their underlying assumptions or before examining the question "What might go wrong with our plan?"

- ✤ Keep the *process* healthy (that is, follow the seven points above) without overly influencing the *content* (that is, the outcomes). If you need to control outcomes, make decisions on your own rather than convene meetings.

- ✤ When the meeting ends, summarize accomplishments and reaffirm commitments to follow up.

We must indeed all hang together, or most assuredly we shall all hang separately.

—BENJAMIN FRANKLIN

Mold individuals into a team.

You'll get better results from your employees if their efforts are united in a single direction by a sense of common interest. You can provide that unification.

Yes, You Can!
❦

§ Hire those job candidates who demonstrate a desire to be team players, rather than "Lone Rangers."

§ State your expectations, in specific, written terms, of how employees will work as team players. *Example:* "Make suggestions for improving the way we serve our customers."

§ Define the team clearly and in writing so everyone knows exactly what team they're on.

§ Conduct regular team meetings during which the team concept is discussed and reinforced.

§ Recognize and reward employees *as a team* when they accomplish something as a team.

§ Show as much appreciation to your second-stringers as you do to your all-stars.

§ Recognize and reward individuals for being good team players as much as for individual excellence. Criticize behavior that weakens team unity. Put an item or two addressing team player skills on the performance review form.

§ Step in to resolve conflicts that threaten solidarity. Make clear how important harmony is to you.

§ Never compare employees to each other or hold up one as a model for the others to emulate.

§ Ensure that team members get to know each other and the nature of each other's responsibilities and duties very well.

§ Model through your actions the very same teamwork you expect of them.

§ Ignite employee passions with a vision that inspires, unites, and focuses.

A community is like a ship;
everyone ought to be prepared
to take the helm.

—Henrik Ibsen

Manage a self-directed team.

The idea behind the self-directed team is to *liberate* a group of workers to do what is required of them. Once team members are shown what the organization expects, they are free, within certain boundaries, to determine the best way to attain those outcomes. You can help a self-directed work team to prosper.

Yes, You Can!
❧

- ❦ For the first self-managed teams in your company, select those members most likely to thrive under this new system, thereby establishing an initial success.

- ❦ Train the team and their supervisors in the self-managed concept. Show them what behavior is required of them. Continue the training even after the team has begun to operate.

- ❦ Provide teams and their supervisors with a clear purpose. Tell them exactly what your rationale is for asking them to function this way. Emphasize the benefits to them. Show them how they'll be contributing more positively to the organization.

- ❦ Give the teams clear expectations of what they are to accomplish and the degree of quality they are to attain. Establish mutually agreed upon measures of success so they can gauge their outcomes.

- ❦ See that the supervisor gives the team frequent feedback on their performance. Make sure they know how they're doing. Particularly in the early days of the team effort, provide whatever assistance workers need to redirect their efforts in a more productive direction.

- ❦ See that team members get an avalanche of positive reinforcement from each other, from supervisors, from upper management, and from customers.

- ❦ Support the supervisors of your teams with coaching and encouragement. Stand behind them.

Training is everything.
The peach was once a bitter
almond; cauliflower is nothing
but a cabbage with a
college education.

—MARK TWAIN

Sponsor useful training.

Many companies spend a great deal of money to train employees. But the investment is not always returned in terms of visible benefits to the bottom line. You can sponsor training in your company that produces valuable results.

Yes, You Can!
ॐ

§ Use performance review results or surveys of superiors, peers, and subordinates to decide what training to provide.

§ Have employees meet with superiors prior to training to agree upon exactly what they should be looking to get out of the experience.

§ Organize shorter sessions spread out over time rather than longer, more concentrated sessions. Five consecutive days of training is not likely to be retained as well or applied as fully as a half-day session held once a week for ten weeks.

§ Ensure that training programs have clearly stated learning objectives, consist of practical examples and applications, provide opportunities for participants to influence the thrust of the content, include activities that *involve* them in their learning, and give plenty of openings to ask questions.

§ Hire the best trainers available. Don't look to save money on them; you usually get what you pay for.

§ Ask participants to evaluate the training they receive and suggest what should be eliminated, added, or improved before it is offered again. Ensure that trainers respond to this feedback.

§ Prior to the end of a training session, have participants construct action plans of how they'll apply what they have learned to doing their job.

§ Insist that participants discuss their action plans with their bosses immediately following the seminar.

CHAPTER 6

PROSPER AT WORK

By working faithfully eight hours a day
you may eventually get to be a boss and
work twelve hours a day.

—ROBERT FROST

It is not enough to be industrious; so are the ants. What are you industrious about?

—HENRY DAVID THOREAU

Find out what your boss expects.

You work for a "puzzle"—one of those bosses who believes he or she hired a psychic. You are expected to read the boss's mind, knowing what is to be done and how to do it. Unless you ask, these secrets won't be revealed to you until it's too late. You *can* unravel the mystery.

Yes, You Can!

⚜

◈ Ask for an up-to-date job description.

◈ You may have a current job description that covers only the scope of your responsibilities—the "what." Explain to your boss that to do your job better you should know the "why," the "how," and "to what degree of quality." Ask that these expectations be written down for each of your duties.

◈ If your boss won't or can't provide you with written expectations, write them yourself. Then submit them for revision and approval. Discuss them to ensure that both of you understand each of them to mean the same thing.

◈ Never leave a puzzle's presence without a contract. When given an assignment, tell your boss exactly how you plan to approach it and what form you expect the results to take. Get approval on your plans now so that you won't later hear "That's not the way I wanted that done!"

◈ Ask other employees about their understanding of the boss's expectations. If one of them has been more effective than you at deciphering the boss's needs, learn from that person's success.

◈ Conduct an intense study of your boss over the next thirty days. Spend a great deal of time in his or her presence. Pay attention. Observe his or her behavior more closely than at any time before. Listen more intently than you ever have. At the end of the thirty days, synthesize what you have learned about what's important to your boss.

A man should live with his superiors as he does with fire: not too near, lest he burn; nor too far off, lest he freeze.

—DIOGENES

Please your boss.

Your job is to serve at the pleasure of your boss. The more pleasurable you make that service, the quicker you'll get to the top. You can find many ways to delight your supervisor.

Yes, You Can!
֍

֍ Each day do something to make your boss look good—especially to his or her boss.

֍ Learn the greatest pains and frustrations your boss experiences; eliminate at least one of them.

֍ See that problems get resolved before they reach the boss's desk. If you must present a problem to the boss, go in armed with possible solutions.

֍ Keep the boss informed. Never let either good news or bad news come from anyone but you.

֍ Praise your boss to others; they are likely to spill the beans on you.

֍ Learn your boss's expectations for your performance. Don't start any new assignment without being absolutely sure you know what the boss is looking for.

֍ Find out what skills he or she considers you to be least adept in; immerse yourself in a professional development program to perfect them.

֍ Save money for your company. Discover ways to do things cheaper.

֍ Make money for your company. Discover new markets or ways to get additional business in old markets.

֍ Be seen as an innovator. Find ways to do things better, faster, and differently.

֍ Take such great care of your customers—both internal and external—that they praise you to the boss.

I don't meet competition.
I crush it.

—CHARLES REVSON

Serve customers exceptionally.

Corporate dynasties have been built on stellar customer service. Federal Express, Disney, Nordstrom's, and Wal-Mart are dramatic and visible examples. *Your* company's name may not yet be a household word, but you can improve your bottom line today through greater responsiveness to the people who pay your salary.

Yes, You Can!

- Remember, you're always either servicing the customer or servicing someone who is servicing the customer. Act like it!

- Treat your employees the way you want them to treat your customers. If you abuse your employees, don't be surprised that they abuse your customers.

- Make your expectations for the treatment of customers exceptionally clear to frontline service providers.

- Anticipate. Anticipate. Anticipate. Don't merely respond to customers. Meet their needs before they ask, and solve their problems before they complain.

- Give your customers far more than they expect.

- Listen intently to complaining customers, and solve their problems quickly, generously, happily, thankfully, and remorsefully.

- Never allow your customers to hear "No," or "That's not my job."

- Communicate with customers. Don't allow them to be punished by unclear policies. Improve the directions you give them as well as any signs you want them to heed. Be scrupulously honest about products and services.

- Gather your employees to brainstorm answers to this question: "How can we serve our customers better, faster, and differently than the competition?"

- Continually ask customers how you're doing. Listen to their answers and act on them.

*It's what you learn after you
know it all that counts.*

—John Wooden

Find out how well you're doing.

Ask most employees what they think about the feedback they receive from their boss, and they will respond, "What feedback?" If this is your dilemma, you can find ways to get your boss to provide constructive criticism about your performance.

Yes, You Can!
❦

- ❧ The next time your boss fails to react to something you do, ask this question: "What's *one thing* I might have done differently to get a better outcome?" This question is more likely to get a helpful response than asking more generally, "How did you like that job I did?"

- ❧ Ask your boss what one thing the *big* boss would say about your performance. The answer is likely to be a flimsily disguised piece of feedback from your boss.

- ❧ Get hold of an employee performance review form, possibly the one used in your company by managers who do give feedback, and ask your boss to use the form to grade your performance. If that doesn't work, complete it yourself and ask your boss for his or her agreement with your self-assessment.

- ❧ Listen to complaints the boss makes about overall performance that aren't directed toward anyone in particular. Ask what you can do to improve in that area, yourself.

- ❧ Ask a close colleague of your boss what your boss thinks of your performance.

- ❧ Ask, "Boss, if you could send me to one training program, what would it be?" Or request your boss's help in creating a long-term professional development plan that includes one-on-one coaching.

- ❧ Don't turn your boss off by blowing up or retreating when you *do* receive criticism.

If you're not fired with enthusiasm you'll be fired with enthusiasm.

—VINCE LOMBARDI

Increase your chances to advance.

A promotion isn't something that just happens; it results from careful planning along the way. You can figure out what it will take for you to get ahead.

Yes, You Can!
ॐ

§ Early in your career ask your boss to help you create a career map that lays out possible routes through the hierarchy. The plan should include the "dues" you must pay in the form of time in grade, professional development, and performance standards. Upgrade the map yearly.

§ Latch on to a mentor—who may or may not be your boss. Write down your career goals, and ask your mentor for advice on how to attain them.

§ Don't push so hard that your salary gets too far out of line for someone in your position. Top management may find it too costly to promote (or *retain*) you.

§ Study the routes that others ahead of you have taken to the top. Emulate them.

§ Remain alert to new openings. Don't depend on your boss, who may be afraid to lose you. Ask for support in your bids for available positions that might help you advance.

§ Without becoming a nuisance or running the risk of being seen as overly ambitious, remind your boss periodically of your interest in upward mobility.

§ Be friendly and helpful to people in positions to which you aspire. They may be asked to recommend a replacement for themselves someday.

§ Establish a reputation outside your company as an expert. This may get you a terrific job offer, and your boss may then see the need to retain you by offering you a promotion.

If I am not for myself, who will
be? If I am only for myself,
what am I?

—Hillel the Elder

Sell yourself effectively.

Your successes will advance your career only if others find out about them. You can keep the people in your company informed about the value of your contributions without blowing your own horn too loudly.

Yes, You Can!

ॐ

§ First, be certain you have a good product to market. Be *very* good at what you do.

§ Keep key decision makers informed on an ongoing basis of developments within your area of expertise that are of interest to the firm.

§ Submit articles for publication in your company's newsletter that highlight your responsibilities and your accomplishments. Offer to write a monthly column.

§ Ask your boss to take you to staff meetings attended by high-ranking company officials. Without being pushy, introduce yourself to any higher-ups you encounter.

§ Ask your boss for opportunities to showcase your presentation skills to upper management. (Sharpen those skills first!)

§ Greet top-level managers whenever and wherever you see them. Use a simple, "Hello, Ms. Roberts." After a while they'll begin asking and finding out who you are.

§ Author, or coauthor with your boss, reports that will have high visibility. Make sure your name appears on the cover.

§ Volunteer for assignments that will bring you into contact with a wide variety of new people both inside and outside the company.

§ Be sure your boss sees any written commendations you receive from customers.

§ Be kind and helpful to as many coworkers as you can, and let word of mouth do the rest.

Value has been defined as the
ability to command the price.

—Louis D. Brandeis

Ask for a raise or a promotion.

You believe you deserve a raise, and your worsening financial position has given you the courage to go for it. Can you ask for a raise in a way that will increase your chances of getting it?

Yes, You Can!

∞

§ Ask for it! You won't get a raise by wishing or hinting.

§ Know exactly how much you want and when. If the boss responds to your request by asking what you think you're worth, state the amount confidently.

§ Justify your request in terms of the value of your contribution to the bottom line. Be specific. Let the boss see how giving you a raise is a good idea.

§ Time the request to coincide with some good news the boss has received or with your having recently put in a particularly exemplary performance.

§ Never base an appeal on your financial need. Performance is the selling factor; however, you *are* wise to point to any past wage freezes that may have led to your being paid less than your value to the firm warrants.

§ If you hear that your performance has not earned a raise, ask what you can do that you haven't been doing. Get specific suggestions that you can incorporate into your future behavior so you'll succeed next time. Ask the boss to agree to review your performance in another six months and to reconsider the raise.

§ Anticipate the most likely objections to your request. Be prepared to dismantle them.

§ If the answer is no, negotiate creatively. What can your boss offer you besides money now? Money at a specified date in the future? Reduced working hours? Days off? Increased benefits? More training? Job reassignment? Large discounts on company products? Ask!

The secret of success is making your vocation your vacation.

—MARK TWAIN

Make your work fun.

Successful people don't hate what they do. Work is not some penance we must pay in order to earn a living. You can have fun as you pursue your profession.

Yes, You Can!

❧

- Talk to people who benefit from your work. The more valuable you realize your service is, the happier you'll feel about providing it.

- Discuss with your boss how you can add to your job by taking on certain new responsibilities.

- Innovate! Invent new products and services. Find better, faster, or different ways of doing things. Dream up ways to save money or make money for your organization. Search for creative solutions to old problems. Take a few exciting risks.

- Bring the same curiosity and vitality to your work that you bring to hobbies and personal interests.

- Open your eyes and ears to the comic events that occur daily in your work. Laugh at yourself; laugh at disaster; don't laugh at others.

- Post a witty, profound, and insightful "Saying of the Month" in your office or in a public place for all to see.

- Apply the latest "toys" to your work. Upgrade your computer; invest in some electronic wizardry that makes your job easier, increases your productivity, and gives you a kick.

- Enroll in a seminar that has the goal of making you feel more empowered and more upbeat about your work.

- Keep a work journal or diary. Record your successes and failures. Whenever you're feeling down, read your entries from a year ago to gain perspective on your current problems and to realize how quickly you'll be able to make light of them.

The french fry is my canvas.

—RAY KROC, FOUNDER OF MCDONALD'S

Find fulfillment at work.

Work has the potential to add to life or subtract from it. It can be heavenly, hellish, or somewhere in between. No matter what the circumstances of your work, you can make your work life more fulfilling.

Yes, You Can!
❧

- § Broaden your vision beyond the job you perform. Find out as much about your company as you can. Learn where you fit in the grand scheme, and look for ways to make your fit a more satisfying one.

- § Volunteer for new and more challenging assignments as soon as they become available. Ask before your boss thinks of someone else.

- § Ask your boss what the two of you can do to raise the level of responsibility and creativity in your present assignment. If you want a more enriched job, ask for it. Make specific suggestions.

- § Expand your capabilities; learn new skills. Enjoy the feeling that you can do your job as well as anyone has ever done it.

- § Take advantage of opportunities to help coworkers succeed. Take newcomers and less experienced employees under your wing. Teach them everything you know. Your excitement will grow as they do.

- § Dream up ideas for doing your job better, faster, and differently. The resulting variety and cost savings will pump you up, as will the appreciation you receive from your superiors and customers.

- § If none of the ideas above do the trick for you, and you're determined to feel better about your vocation, start hunting for a new situation that meets your needs to grow while you work.

Manners are like zero in arithmetic. They may not be much in themselves, but they are capable of adding a great deal of value to everything else.

—FREYA STARK

Practice business etiquette.

The golden rule is as important in business as anywhere. Treat people with respect and consideration, and they'll return the favor. Furthermore, there are certain rules of conduct in business that others have every reason to expect you will follow. You can meet these expectations.

Yes, You Can!

ॐ

- ৬ Return phone calls within twenty-four hours. When the person answers, ask, "Is this a good time for you to talk?"

- ৬ When holding a meeting in your office, have your incoming calls held. If there's a vital call you need to take, explain this to your guests in advance.

- ৬ Don't keep appointments waiting without a personal explanation and a sincere apology.

- ৬ Answer letters within ten days. Respond to every request in them.

- ৬ Get to meetings on time; don't monopolize discussions. If you lead meetings, start them and end them on time.

- ৬ When making presentations, don't go even one minute over the allotted time.

- ৬ Introduce people properly. Present the younger/lower-ranking person to the older/higher-ranking person.

- ৬ Address doctors, judges, military officers, academics, and elected officials by their proper title.

- ৬ Remain sensitive to the culture, religious laws, and diet of international visitors and colleagues. Study the practices of other nations before you visit them.

- ৬ Get a book on table manners for business meals.

- ৬ RSVP within one week to all invitations.

- ৬ Write thank-you notes to acknowledge any thoughtful act.

Time is the coin of your life. It is the only coin you have, and only you can determine how it will be spent. Be careful lest you let other people spend it for you.

—CARL SANDBURG

Get organized.

Disorganization is a major contributor to stress and one of the reasons we don't achieve our goals. You can avoid the diseases of clutter, poor planning, and disarray.

Yes, You Can!

⅏

- Make time to organize. Set yearly goals, monthly objectives, and weekly priorities.

- Don't start a new task until you have everything you need—information, supplies, and so on—to get it underway.

- Plan ahead. Lay out the subtasks needed over the coming weeks in order to accomplish a master task.

- Keep a "to do" list with tasks listed according to their value: A = high; B = medium; C = low. Work on only high value tasks. Update your list at the end of the day.

- Do one of four things whenever you pick up a piece of paper—pitch it, send it to someone else, act on it, or file it. Never put it down without performing one of these actions.

- Sort the papers you need into file folders marked "to do," "to file," and "to read." Pitch the rest.

- Stop being a collector. Put away papers, files, and other desk clutter that you haven't looked at for two weeks.

- Divide complex projects into manageable pieces. Attack the project piece by piece. Solve one problem at a time.

- Write down every promise you make and everything you need to remember right away—never on slips of paper, always using a scheduling system and notetaking procedure that works for you. On this "master list" note the tasks you'll complete today.

- Maintain an appointment calendar. Use a coordinated system to keep track of projects.

- Keep your desktop cleared for action.

Dost thou love life? Then do
not squander time, for that is
the stuff that life is made of.

—Benjamin Franklin

Stop wasting time.

Often without thought, we allow time wasters to gobble up chunks of our day. You can prevent these "minute maulers" from doing their damage.

Yes, You Can!

๛

- When planning a new activity, anticipate all that might go wrong so that you won't be forced to fight fires when an unexpected crisis occurs.

- Don't answer the telephone during a meeting or project if it disturbs the flow of progress or causes you to waste other people's time.

- Keep your desk and office organized so you have quick access to what you need. Put things in a place where you won't have to hunt for them.

- Delegate effectively so you are not busier than your subordinates and can make the best use of your time.

- Communicate with the intent *to be understood* so that you don't have to send the same message twice.

- Improve your listening skills so that you'll never be paralyzed by uncertainty about what someone has asked of you.

- See that the meetings you attend start and end on time and that there are no unnecessary deviations from the agenda.

- Stop smoking. You may spend hours each week buying cigarettes, hunting for them, lighting them, taking drags, flicking ashes, snuffing them out, emptying ashtrays, coughing, and reading articles about cancer.

- Stand up when unwanted visitors get past the pit bull who should guard your office. Come around from behind your desk and meet the person near your door.

- Stop thinking about what you have to do and *do it.*

Prosper at Work

Know the true value of time;
snatch, seize, and enjoy
every moment of it.

—Philip Dormer Stanhope

Make good use of time.

Most of us need to find a way to get more out of the hours available to us. It can be done, and *you* can do it.

Yes, You Can!

❧

- Spend time like money; use it to do what is important to you, not what other people tell you is important.

- Examine your daily life routines that can be altered or dispensed with for immediate time savings. *Example:* reading the *entire* newspaper every morning.

- Save your most challenging work for the times of day when you are freshest and at your best.

- Twice a day ask yourself, "Am I making the best use of my time right now?" Change tasks if you aren't.

- Look at your watch frequently to assess the effectiveness of your time-management skills.

- Write less; phone more.

- Outline topics to discuss on the telephone. Make telephone appointments. Open conversations with "What can I do for you?" not "How are you?" Bring calls to a prompt close after completing your business.

- Get to work earlier than others or stay later to profit from uninterrupted productivity. During the day do some of your work away from the office for the same reason.

- Don't take over projects because others are not doing their jobs. Instead, teach or empower them to produce.

- Write answers to letters in the margins of the ones you receive.

- Discontinue unnecessary meetings; see that the ones you must attend are conducted more efficiently.

- Don't overdo revisions when the cost of redoing the work exceeds the value of the improvement gained.

Don't serve time;
make time serve you.

—WILLIE SUTTON

Use waiting time productively.

How much time do you spend standing in line, stalled in traffic, sitting on airplanes, waiting for an appointment or a meeting to begin, being put on hold, or in any one of the hundreds of ways life places you in suspended animation? Even if the time you spend waiting averages only fifteen minutes a day, this could easily consume over two hundred days of your lifetime. You can make better use of this time.

Yes, You Can!

❦

§ Regard waiting as a gift of time, not as a disruption to your productivity. Take advantage of this gift.

§ If you typically find yourself with large chunks of waiting time, enroll in a home-study college course.

§ Keep a good book by your side. Catch up on your pleasure and business reading.

§ Buy a notebook computer so you can be productive away from the office, even where there's no electricity.

§ Take work with you wherever you go. Do tasks that you don't normally find the time to do when you're at your office. Update your "to do" list or calendar. Set goals for next year.

§ Take a refreshing catnap. (Not in traffic!)

§ Let your mind wander through a task you're tackling. Visualize your progress and the next steps you'll take. Dream of new ways to attack the problem. Ask what-if and why-not questions.

§ Carry a small pad and a pen with you at all times to record ideas you get while on the run.

§ Learn while you drive. Use time stuck in traffic to improve your mind with educational audiotapes.

§ Work on one task while waiting for another to be completed. *Example:* Make a phone call while your computer or printer completes a routine.

A committee of three
gets things done if two
don't show up.

—HERBERT V. PROCHNOW

Stand out at meetings.

You may not run every meeting you attend, but you can be an active participant and thereby contribute significantly to what gets accomplished.

Yes, You Can!
∾

§ Arrive on time, with agenda in hand. Don't miss meetings without prior notification/approval.

§ Stop doing any personal work as soon as the meeting begins.

§ Stick to the agenda and to the task at hand at any given moment. Build on the present discussion rather than changing the focus to your own interests.

§ Be positive. Maintain a problem-solving not a blame-placing posture; focus on the future rather than getting mired in the past. Focus on what *can* be done, rather than agonizing over the group's limitations.

§ Participate, speak up, and be candid, but don't monopolize the meeting. Encourage your colleagues to do the same.

§ When the meeting leader is failing to move the group in a productive direction, suggest ways to get the meeting back on track without threatening the leader.

§ Challenge bad ideas; present better ones. Don't attack people in the process.

§ Perform any agreed upon, between-meeting follow-up tasks within twenty-four hours.

§ Never leak confidential discussions to outsiders.

§ Report back immediately to those who count on being briefed by you regarding the outcomes of the meeting.

§ Whenever the group makes a democratic decision that goes against your judgment, say so. But once your exception is noted, support the group's decision to the hilt.

The training which makes men happiest in themselves also makes them most serviceable to others.

—JOHN RUSKIN

Choose the best seminars for you.

These days training companies and consultants offer an overwhelming selection of professional development opportunities. You can choose the best ones for you.

Yes, You Can!

෨

- Review your most recent performance reviews and identify deficiencies that might be addressed in a seminar.

- Ask your boss for suggestions.

- Define clearly what you want out of a seminar. Are you attracted by learning? Networking? Do you want to acquire specific skills? Certification? Something else?

- Read the brochure carefully. Is it sleazy or classy? Do the benefits of attending sound attractive to you? Does the outline look relevant to your needs? Is certification offered in your field? Are you identified in the "who should attend" section?

- Call the sponsoring organization. Find out how many times the speaker has conducted this seminar. Ask for a list of past participants you can call. Be aware of how well the organization handles your questions.

- Check into the reputation of the sponsor and the speaker. Are they well known in the field? Is a guarantee of satisfaction provided?

- Call the speaker. Ask about the format. Is it all lecture? Will the attendees form small working groups? Role-play? Does the schedule allow time for questions and answers? How do you feel about his or her responses?

- Find out how many people are likely to attend. Lower-priced seminars may attract hundreds—great for networking, but not so great if you are relying on individual attention.

- Decide whether the fee seems to correlate with your perception of the quality of the program. Don't pay too much. Don't search for bargains.

The shy man will not learn; the impatient man should not teach. Ask and learn.

—HILLEL THE ELDER

Get the most out of a seminar.

Those who profit the most from seminars *plan* their approach to this learning opportunity. You, too, can get more out of the seminars you attend.

Yes, You Can!

- Before you go, talk to your boss or someone else with whom you can set goals for gaining specific new skills.

- Prior to the seminar read a book on the topic and preview whatever materials are made available by the instructor. Arrive ready to hit the ground learning.

- Be sure you know how to find the seminar location. Arrive thirty minutes early. Introduce yourself to the instructor and to other participants. Build a network of contacts.

- Be an active participant. Consider the meeting room a laboratory where you will try new behaviors, take risks, and engage in self-discovery.

- Avoid doing business during breaks. Let your office know that you won't be available to take calls.

- Take notes and resolve to review them within twenty-four hours and then once a week until you have achieved your learning goals.

- Connect what you learn to *yourself*. Don't think, "So-and-so needs to hear this." So-and-so is not at the seminar. You're there to clean up your own act.

- Build an action plan. At each break write down those ideas that you might implement in your daily work.

- Meet with your boss the first day back on the job. Reveal your new ideas. Ask your boss to identify which strategies should have priority, and get your boss to support your putting them into practice. Request an ongoing coaching relationship.

There is no future in any job.
The future lies in the man
who holds the job.

—GEORGE CRANE

Survive a reorganization.

Hanging on to your job following a takeover or the downsizing of your company is a blessing. But the immediate aftermath can be stressful and fraught with uncertainty. Can you do something to improve your morale, productivity, and ability to survive this uneasy period?

Yes, You Can!
☙

- ৡ Don't wallow in guilt over friends who are gone. You'll need to be at your best to survive the next round of cutbacks.

- ৡ Stay out of the grapevine. Top management will think less of your trustworthiness if they get wind of criticisms you have of the changes that you are unwilling to state openly.

- ৡ While having concerns about your job security is natural, don't become paranoid. If you're losing sleep about your future, seek counseling, request assurances from top management, or find another job.

- ৡ Find the opportunity in this adversity. Can you make a career gain in the midst of this instability? Can you offer a special service the company needs right now, and increase your value?

- ৡ Don't waste your energy looking for scapegoats. The "bad guys" in this scenario are changing markets, the need to stay close to customers, or worsening financial conditions. Negativity, anger, and resentment will hurt your chances to survive.

- ৡ Become a spokesperson for hope, renewal, and better times. When coworkers preach gloom and doom, chime in with optimism. Point to the sun behind the clouds. You'll help yourself, energize them, and gain points in the boardroom.

- ৡ Work toward the future. This may or may not be the end of the corporate upheaval. Continue to develop your skills and increase your options. Five years from now the details of today will be insignificant.

There is no security on this earth; there is only opportunity.

—Douglas MacArthur

Increase your job security.

Fellow employees are falling like flies in the midst of a corporate downsizing. You love your job and want to make sure you'll keep it. Can you take out an insurance policy for job security?

Yes, You Can!

❧

- Choose a job in an occupation where rapid growth is projected in the coming years.

- Go to work for a smaller company. Financial adversity is less likely to trigger layoffs in a mom-and-pop shop than in a corporate behemoth.

- Become the best at what you do, and indispensable.

- Be seen as a team player who seeks to promote the company more than yourself. Be willing to move laterally as well as vertically to benefit the firm.

- Work for the unit in your company that contributes the most to the bottom line or is most vital to the company's mission.

- Make your unit more successful and therefore more vital to the company.

- Find out what's hot in your field and become an expert at it. Stay on top of new developments.

- Find out what's important to the CEO and become the most reliable supplier of it. Recommend cost-saving or income-producing measures.

- Work for a powerful and respected boss who is not likely to receive the largest staffing hits.

- Make your boss look good—continually.

- Make no enemies. A scorned coworker might be in a position someday to engineer your demise.

- Be a good friend. A close colleague might be in the position to give higher-ups an opinion of your value to the firm.

Experience is not what happens to a man, it's what a man does with what happens to him.

—ALDOUS HUXLEY

Survive a job loss.

Your world just fell apart. The job you were counting on to last for years is no longer yours. Can you endure?

Yes, You Can!
ॐ

§ Negotiate the best severance package you can get. Develop a bare-bones house budget. Consider taking out loans from relatives or, if necessary, declaring bankruptcy.

§ Expect to experience these emotional stages: disbelief, betrayal, anger, embarrassment, and panic. Engage in self-talk at each stage, accepting the emotion, but not allowing it to last any longer than necessary or to cause you to do anything foolish.

§ Consider getting professional help if the emotional burden becomes too great or if it appears that a job search firm or vocational counselor might offer some assistance.

§ Let your family provide emotional support. Don't allow embarrassment to create distance between you and them.

§ As soon as you're ready to plan for a new job, spend at least a day or two considering the possibility of a complete change in career. Perhaps you were in the wrong field. You may have gifts that can be parlayed into a new vocation that might be more fulfilling and lucrative.

§ Make a list of everyone who can assist you with your job search. Call on them, starting with those who are most likely to be helpful.

§ Don't bad-mouth the company or the person who fired you. They may be back in your employment picture someday.

§ Before you get too far into your new job, ask yourself why you really lost your last one. If there was one thing you did to contribute to your demise, what was it? What will you do to prevent yourself from making the same mistake?

Success is a matter of luck.
Ask any failure.

—EARL WILSON

Conduct a smart job hunt.

With more people chasing fewer jobs, you need to increase the probability that you'll find a position that will advance your career. Can you shop for a job more wisely?

Yes, You Can!
❦

- ❧ If your job hunt is dictated by the loss of a job, take some time to calm down, assess the situation, and examine your options. Don't jump into a job search until your emotions are settled and you have performed a thorough self-analysis.

- ❧ Prepare a well-organized, tastefully designed résumé. Impress prospective employers by using some of these words: *teamwork, motivation, diversity, profits, quality, safety, cost-cutting,* and *solutions.* Cite specific accomplishments that helped to improve your former employer's bottom line.

- ❧ Don't expect results from a mass mailing. Use your résumé as a leave-behind piece or as a calling card.

- ❧ Contact people who might assist you in your job search. Ask them to do what they can to help you. Most of them may not be able to get you an interview, but ask for an appointment to pick their brains for job-hunting ideas and to learn about solid job leads.

- ❧ Look for opportunities to network at seminars, professional meetings, and conventions.

- ❧ Have a friend posing as a potential employer check that each of your references extolls your virtues.

- ❧ Wait ten days before responding to a help-wanted ad. The prejudice of many employers is that the second wave of applications is of higher quality than the first.

- ❧ When you find a company where you really want to work, express your enthusiasm and tell the employer that you're willing to wait for an opening. As time passes, keep in touch. Your persistence may be rewarded.

The closest to perfection a
person ever becomes is
when he fills out a job
application form.

—STANLEY J. RANDALL

Ace an interview.

When two candidates have similar credentials, the one who is better at selling him- or herself usually gets the job. You can convince an interviewer that you are too good to pass up.

Yes, You Can!
❧

- § Prepare thoroughly. Show a complete knowledge of the company and ask probing, but not rude or invasive, questions about current corporate issues.

- § Don't do the following: appear aggressive or submissive; use first names unless asked to; smoke, even if invited; sit down before asked to; look at your watch; show anxiety or boredom; ask about salary or benefits; answer questions before the interviewer has finished asking them.

- § When asked, be crystal clear on your career objectives.

- § When asked why you left your last job, claim insufficient challenge, no room for advancement, that you were underpaid, or that the company was not stable or was losing its edge. *Never criticize your past boss.*

- § When asked to talk about yourself, cite specific examples of your outstanding accomplishments.

- § When asked about your weaknesses, identify a strength that you are committed to improving. (Presentation skills is a good choice.) Don't criticize yourself.

- § Practice answers to questions you hope won't come up.

- § Practice your table etiquette for interviews over meals.

- § Mirror the tone of voice and body language of the interviewer; sit in the same posture.

- § When you're not speaking, *listen.*

- § Ask for the job! Say, "I'd very much like to work for you. If you invite me to join your team, I won't let you down."

CHAPTER 7

PROSPER AT HOME

Where we love is home—home that our
feet may leave, but not our hearts.

—OLIVER WENDELL HOLMES, SR.

Less is more.

—ROBERT BROWNING

Simplify your life.

Expanding cable service makes channel-surfing more frustrating. Your automobile is a technological marvel, but the automatic antenna won't retract anymore. Your battery-run appliances are great, but you can never remember to recharge them. Your job demands half of your life. You get more magazines than you can read. Every night of your week is committed. Can you get back control of your life?

Yes, You Can!

ॐ

- Remember that you have choices. No one holds a gun to your head and says you *must* complicate your life.

- Keep needs versus wants in perspective. Do you mistakenly believe that you *need* that exotic new electronic gear, when in fact you only *want* it?

- Cut back on the complexity and expense of your lifestyle so you can transfer to a lower-paying and less-demanding job.

- Learn how to say no. When your boss piles on the work, ask what is important enough to be done in the time you have to do it and what can wait.

- Take stock of how much what you do benefits you directly and how much you do for others (for example, your children) that they ought to learn to do for themselves.

- Reduce the number of gadgets in your life. When your garage-door opener breaks down, disconnect it. Make coffee on the stove. Pull out your answering machine. Limit the options on your next car. Weed out magazine subscriptions.

- Don't "do it yourself"; pay someone else to do it.

- Learn to say no when you are asked to help, volunteer for, or join a group or cause.

- Put aside one hour each day during which you'll do only what you want to do, not what the world tells you to do.

I've been rich and I've been poor—rich is better.

—SOPHIE TUCKER

Save money.

Some people never seem to have enough money—the more they make, the more difficult it is to hang on to it. You can stop squandering your hard-earned income.

Yes, You Can!
୧୬

§ Pay no more in taxes than you have to. Devour self-help tax books; get professional tax advice.

§ If possible, sell your car and instead use a combination of public transportation, taxis, and rental cars.

§ Shop for a bank or investment agency with the lowest service charges and with the highest rates of return.

§ Invest windfalls in lowering your mortgage principal to lower the total interest you'll pay; avoid large impulse buys.

§ Cut up your credit cards, or always pay off the balance before interest is charged to your account.

§ Stop visiting the mall as a pastime; go only when you need something; refuse to buy anything that is not on sale.

§ Make what you have last longer. Change the oil in your car more often and keep your car in a garage; dust the coils of your refrigerator; remove good clothing as soon as you come home; hold on to everything 25 percent longer.

§ Buy the right thing in the right place. Learn what is cheapest in the supermarket, what to buy in the discount warehouse, and what items are priced the same everywhere. Clip manufacturer's and retailer's coupons.

§ Negotiate. You'll be surprised how many cash-starved retailers are willing to give discounts to those who ask for them.

§ Buy things used or slightly damaged. Visit thrift stores, consignment shops, garage sales, and large flea markets. Ask for irregulars in factory outlets; request blemished auto tires; buy day-old baked goods.

Keep thy eyes wide open before marriage, and half-shut afterwards.

—BENJAMIN FRANKLIN

Choose a compatible mate.

Divorce is painful—unhappy marriages are worse. It will be tough enough to make a life with another person if you pick the *right* person. Don't start married life with two strikes against the two of you. You can avoid this irreversible error.

Yes, You Can!

୭

- Before you marry, think long and hard about what marriage means to you. *Why* are you getting married? To eliminate a deficit in your existence (for example, loneliness), or to enjoy life more fully by sharing it with someone else? The latter is a healthier reason.

- What explicit expectations do you have for a spouse? Are there any behaviors you insist upon? What kind of relationship are you hoping for? Discuss the answers to these questions with your future spouse.

- Over a period of weeks discuss the expectations both of you have for marriage. Decide what's really important, resolve any differences, and negotiate to the point where you can willingly buy into each other's expectations before you tie the knot.

- Marry based on compatibility, caring, and common values. Slight adjustments in these areas may be possible, but don't hope for, or expect, major changes.

- Do you like *everything* about the way your future spouse has treated you before you decided to get married? If not, remember: it won't get any better after the ceremony.

- What do you enjoy more—the things you do for your prospective spouse or the things that he or she does for you? The future looks bright for the two of you if you each respond to this question by saying, "The things I do for her [him]."

- Can you say with confidence that you're looking forward to growing old with this person?

Marriage resembles a pair of shears, so joined that they cannot be separated, often moving in opposite directions, yet always punishing anyone who comes between them.

—SYDNEY SMITH

Have a happy marriage.

The bliss of marriage is having a partner with whom to share life's intimate joys and sorrows. But maintaining a strong and healthy union is a difficult challenge. If they are not careful, a man and woman once very close can slowly drift apart. Can you keep this from happening to you?

Yes, You Can!
⚘

- Listen! In the evening ask your spouse to share the day's experiences with you *before* you do the same. Give your undivided attention. Respond to the feelings that are expressed—don't reject any of them.

- Half of the mistakes made in the relationship will be yours. Apologize when you make them, but don't think that a mere apology ever lets you off the hook. Make a commitment to your partner not to repeat the mistake. Fulfill that commitment.

- Make up after fights. Be the first to seek reconciliation. Send a note or call your spouse at/from work. Either apologize or merely say, "I'm sorry we had such a terrible fight."

- Support your spouse. Be his or her blocker, coach, and cheerleader. Lift your spouse up to the world.

- Never criticize the one you love to others. Never ridicule him or her—anytime, anyplace. Never threaten or tell your spouse to get out, unless you mean it—for good.

- Ask for feedback on how you're doing. On a regular basis discuss what each of you could be doing more of, less of, and equally for each other. Don't harbor unexpressed negative feelings; these are the seeds of alienation and separation.

- Touch your partner constantly, with hugs, rubs, and holding hands. Hang on to intimacy for dear life.

- Renew your wedding vows where you were married or in a special place in the presence of loved ones.

If we had paid no more
attention to our plants
than we have to our children,
we would now be living in a
jungle of weeds.

—LUTHER BURBANK

Be a better parent.

There may be no greater opportunity to influence the world positively than through the children you raise. Can you provide your children with a healthy upbringing?

Yes, You Can!
∾

- ☙ Spend at least fifteen minutes each day talking to your children; find out what's on their minds.

- ☙ Tell them about your job; talk about your workday.

- ☙ Lead by example, not exhortation; communicate your values by deed, not by laying down the law.

- ☙ Assign children meaningful household duties; teach them how to contribute to the upkeep of *their* home.

- ☙ Teach them financial responsibility; make them earn at least a portion of the money they need/want for special purchases, activities, family vacations, and college.

- ☙ Watch for trouble signs: changes in friends, values, weight, routine, or mood. Take threats of suicide seriously, and seek counseling for your child the same day.

- ☙ Don't ignore your own welfare, or that of your spouse, by getting totally absorbed in your children's lives.

- ☙ Say "I'm sorry" when you've hurt them; admit when you're wrong.

- ☙ Accept that your children aren't carbon copies of you; don't expect them to respond to life in the same ways you have.

- ☙ Endure the stage they may go through of being embarrassed to be seen with you.

- ☙ Pay attention to positive behavior; praise it so children will repeat it.

- ☙ Arrange for *responsible* adult supervision when you're not there.

- ☙ Leave detailed instructions in your will outlining how you want your children to be raised.

There is no friendship, no love,
like that of the parent for
the child.

—HENRY WARD BEECHER

Be a better stepparent.

This is the era of the blended family. More and more men and women enter into second marriages with husband and wife bringing their own children to the union. Being a successful stepparent is a challenge, but it's one you can handle.

Yes, You Can!
୰

- During the courtship of your next spouse, don't romance the kids. Don't lavish excessive attention on them, but do show them how happy you are to be marrying them, too.

- Expect to be resented, especially if the other parent is still alive. Even if that parent has died, the children may feel that you are taking their mother or father away from them, probably because they got lots of attention between the end of the previous marriage and your arrival on the scene.

- Resolve the issue of what name the children will use to address you. Tell the kids you would be proud if they would call you Mom (Dad), but that you'll understand if that's something they may not be able to do.

- Watch your own children for signs that they feel you favor your new spouse over them. Reserve a special time each day just for them. Ask them how things are going.

- Talk a lot about the issue of child discipline with your spouse and come to an agreement about exactly how to handle it.

- If you see your spouse's children being manipulative or disrespectful with your spouse, don't unilaterally rush to his or her rescue. Be patient. Tell your spouse what you see, and come up with a joint plan for how to handle the children.

- Talk with your spouse for a few minutes each night about how well each of you is doing.

There are only two lasting bequests we can hope to give our children. One of these is roots; the other, wings.

—HODDING CARTER, JR.

Raise positive, successful children.

Adult attitudes are shaped during childhood. Negative adults may have grown up in pessimistic environments with grumbling parents. Positive adults were probably reared by upbeat parents in emotionally supportive homes. You can help your children develop a positive outlook.

Yes, You Can!

- Teach your children to express emotional distress and pain rather than sit on their feelings.

- Dish out lots of positive reinforcement. When you do, praise your children's deeds, not them, so as not to connect their self-esteem to their performance. In the same way, when you criticize, condemn the deed, not the doer.

- Respond to expressions of fear by asking your children to talk about what they are feeling; share similar anxieties you had at their age.

- Accept their emotions as real. Never criticize, ridicule, or make light of their feelings.

- Lavish attention on older siblings when a new baby arrives.

- Don't smother children with protection and control.

- Give them privacy without letting them become reclusive.

- When they are infants, respond quickly to their cries and give them lots of physical love.

- Listen to your children. Don't make them wait to share something important with you; at the same time, teach them that their needs won't always be met on demand.

- Be their sex educator before the "streets" take over.

- If you love your work, let your children know.

- Let your children witness expressions of warmth and caring and displays of affection between you and your spouse.

What we want to see is the child in pursuit of knowledge, and not knowledge in pursuit of the child.

—GEORGE BERNARD SHAW

Help children learn.

Parents can no longer take education for granted. Both your children and your schools need you to become an active partner in your children's schooling. You can play a vital role in your children's future.

Yes, You Can!

❧

- ❧ Buy your children educational toys when they're young.

- ❧ Don't be a commercial TV addict. If you limit your viewing time, it will be easier for you to limit theirs.

- ❧ Train them to be readers: read to them beginning in infancy; give them books as gifts throughout their lives; let them see you reading and enjoying books.

- ❧ Hold home spelling quizzes and other tests for prizes.

- ❧ Train your children to ask questions at an early age; be receptive to them; praise their inquisitiveness.

- ❧ Teach them the importance of putting in an effort and not to focus so much on results. Discourage them from equating their self-esteem with their grades; appreciate good report cards, but don't make a big deal about them.

- ❧ Don't enroll them sooner than necessary in elementary school; bright kids are often weak socializers.

- ❧ Visit teachers; discuss the curriculum.

- ❧ Show your appreciation to teachers; ask how you can help, but don't become a bother to them. Back up good teachers; praise them to your children.

- ❧ Scan teacher rosters for the coming school year; speak up when it appears that a teaching assignment has been made for administrative expedience rather than the children's benefit.

- ❧ Consider the possibility of homeschooling if the time and talent are available between you and your spouse.

- ❧ Start saving today for your children's college tuition.

You can learn many things
from children. How much
patience you have, for instance.

—FRANKLIN P. JONES

Discipline children constructively.

Most parents handle discipline in one of three ways. Some do it harshly; some don't do it at all; others have discovered how to mete it out in an effective fashion. You can learn the secrets of effective disciplining.

Yes, You Can!
&

- Make no empty threats or weak statements about what you don't want them to do.

- Make no real threats; don't yell or nag.

- Pick your fights carefully; don't discipline excessively or over trivial matters.

- Don't allow tantrums to escalate; call a truce when either side needs to cool off. To calm down, put your feelings in writing.

- Never hit your children. You can correct children's behavior by teaching them self-discipline; this will not be accomplished by physical force.

- Never resort to bribery to get your way.

- When criticizing, say what you see. Don't brand a room full of toys a "mess"; call it what it is: a room full of toys.

- Make no "you" statements. Make plenty of "I" statements—to express feelings more than to demand compliance.

- When you criticize an action, say what's wrong with it. Don't simply insist on having your way.

- When corrective action is required, enlist your child in devising a plan. ("What can we do to be sure this doesn't happen again?")

- After you deliver discipline, hug your child. Express unconditional love, even as you reject the behavior that triggered the discipline.

In a united family, happiness
springs of itself.

— CHINESE PROVERB

Create a close-knit family.

The family remains *the* fundamental support group in our social fabric. However, in many ways the forces of modern society act to pull the family apart. Can you hold your family together?

Yes, You Can!

❧

- § If possible, give your first child at least one brother or sister.

- § When children are young, make your expectations for establishing a "family team" clearly known.

- § Encourage your family to support, defend, and protect each other in public, even as they disagree in private.

- § Never take sides in fights, but step in as an impartial facilitator to help resolve them.

- § Hold weekly family meetings; create a climate where feelings can be openly discussed. Make sure that the youngest members are listened to as seriously as the oldest ones.

- § Consult the whole family when making important decisions— from choosing a pet to planning a vacation.

- § Demand respect for every family member, regardless of age or infirmity. Discipline disrespectful behavior, especially when it is directed at parents or grandparents.

- § Schedule fun family events from the time the children are young. Take your children with you more often than you leave them with a baby-sitter.

- § Continue taking family vacations for as long as possible.

- § Expose your children to the extended family. Give them plenty of opportunities to relate to grandparents, aunts and uncles, and cousins.

- § Hold family reunions each year.

- § Take your children to weekly religious worship beginning at an early age.

One should no more be
affectionate in front of a child
without including him than eat
in front of him while he
remains hungry.

—ERIC BERNE

Express family love more fully.

When you treasure someone, you want it to show. As that person experiences your devotion, you're likely to get equal doses of caring in return. You can learn ways to declare your love for family members in unequivocal terms.

Yes, You Can!

- Listen to the people you love when they come to you with problems, concerns, or fears.

- Through your actions show the people you love that your relationship with them is more important to you than your job, your hobbies, and your possessions.

- Give your *time* to them: time is the most precious gift you can give. Say, "Let's do something together," and then follow through.

- Ask them to talk about what's happening in their lives.

- Say, "I love you" often, with feeling, and at the most unexpected times.

- Display lots of physical affection, especially when you haven't seen each other for an extended period of time.

- Take care of the people you love when they are ill.

- Share your most powerful feelings and most protected emotions.

- Show an interest and get involved in activities (for example, hobbies) that are important to others in your family.

- Show your respect for the people you love by soliciting their ideas and opinions and then acting on them.

- *Feel* how deeply you love the people you live with, and then let your involuntary and uncontrollable nonverbal cues (for example, eyes, face, gestures) take over and say it for you.

- Share a deep faith with the people you love.

These are thy glorious works,
Parent of good.

—JOHN MILTON

Get along with adult children.

In some ways it is more challenging to be the parent of adults than to raise young children. You have to change your attitude and your behavior; in effect, you have to grow up with your kids. Can you do it?

Yes, You Can!

෧

- Do this *before* they become adults: change the way you relate to them to match their advancing emotional age; give them opportunities to make mistakes; set up a timetable for their emancipation.

- Share your opinions in a nonthreatening, take-it-or-leave-it spirit.

- Let them stand on their own, but be there to help.

- Accept them as adults and friends. Find new outlets for the energy you once devoted to child rearing.

- Make sure they are aware of how much you love and appreciate them. Write letters and call them on the phone to remind them.

- Accept their life choices, even after you let them know you may not agree with them.

- If you plan to help them financially, don't withhold the help until they no longer need it or so that they receive it after you're gone.

- Don't feel entitled to a certain frequency of contact with your kids. You won't encourage more communication by making them feel guilty for not calling or stopping by.

- Don't complain constantly to your children about your health or other problems. While you shouldn't hide your adversities from them, or your need for their help, project an image of strength and independence. They need to feel that you're taking good care of yourself.

When I was a boy of fourteen, my father was so ignorant I could hardly stand to have the old man around. But when I got to be twenty-one, I was astonished at how much he had learned in seven years.

—MARK TWAIN

Be a valued son or daughter.

Children don't often give a lot of thought to their relationship with their parents. When they do, they discover wonderful opportunities to repay parents for fulfilling their solemn obligation. You can do the same.

Yes, You Can!

∾

- Don't take advantage of your parents. Do everything possible to avoid infringing on their lives after you should have moved out for good.

- Give your parents the solitude they want but may not ask for. Older parents have the same need for privacy they had when they were young. They still make love, share precious moments, and engage in other forms of intimacy.

- Introduce them to your friends; help your parents to feel a part of your life.

- While you're still living with your parents, assume regular responsibilities for chores around the house. Help them out.

- Ask them for advice. This will make your parents feel useful, and you'll benefit from their years of experience.

- When you disagree with them, do so openly but respectfully. Make it clear that your disagreement in no way diminishes the esteem in which you hold them.

- Surprise them on anniversaries, cook for them, send them on vacations, and do other nice things for them.

- Maintain close and warm relations with your siblings. A close-knit family is a source of support for you and a source of satisfaction for your parents.

- After you move out of the house, stay in close communication with them. Call, write, and visit often. Bring your family to spend the holidays with your parents.

A grandmother is a person with too much wisdom to let that stop her from making a fool of herself over her grandchildren.

—PHIL MOSS

Be a better grandparent.

Grandparenting is more than a role; it is a responsibility. Children benefit from the emotional support, guidance, and love that is available in an extended family. You can fulfill a critical role in the lives of your grandchildren.

Yes, You Can!

֍

- Offer your children any parenting suggestions they request, but don't force unwanted advice on them. Let them make their own mistakes. Share your ideas tentatively so as not to make them feel inadequate as parents.

- Adopt a hands-on approach with your grandchildren; bond with them early in their lives. Take your grandchildren places without their parents on occasion. Create your own relationship with them.

- Leave disciplining to parents, and support them in it.

- Be a teacher, confidant, and supporter.

- If you live far away, send your grandchildren audio- and videotapes with special messages from you. Write letters often.

- Allow each child to be an individual. Don't expect children to mirror you, their parents, or each other.

- Never let grandchildren hear you compare one to the other. Don't give one a nickname that diminishes the others. *Example:* Don't call one your "special guy." Be prepared for jealousy from older grandchildren when you lavish attention on the latest arrival.

- Don't take sides in family squabbles, but always be available to listen to hurts.

- Never criticize your children in front of their children.

- If you live with your children, respect their privacy, don't complain about the food or your living conditions, help with household chores, handle your own finances, and provide the family with treats now and then.

To be seventy years young is
sometimes far more cheerful
and hopeful than to be
forty years old.

—OLIVER WENDELL HOLMES, JR.

Enjoy your retirement.

For some, retirement is the most enjoyable stage of life; for others, it is an empty state of existence. The choice is yours. You can choose to find fulfillment in retirement.

Yes, You Can!

൭

- ৡ Begin making financial plans for a comfortable retirement today! Seek professional counsel and make a commitment to securing your fiscal future. If you're starting late, build retirement capital by working an extra five or six years.

- ৡ Don't allow work to become the central purpose of your life. Some who *do* fail to physically survive as few as six months of retirement. Others who work past their retirement age may miss out on the indescribable joys that life has in store for those with time to celebrate it.

- ৡ Develop hobbies and interests that you can expand during retirement. Plan to volunteer your skills in the community. Commit your energies to a social cause dear to you.

- ৡ Renegotiate roles with the people at home. How can you use your newfound time to help out?

- ৡ Consider starting a business in your home. Get a book on home business opportunities.

- ৡ Try things you have never experienced before. You may discover a talent you never knew you had.

- ৡ Telephone and write letters to all the friends you never had time to keep in touch with.

- ৡ Talk to other retirees to learn from their experiences. Get involved with a group or organization of retirees who stay active and have fun.

- ৡ Take time to enjoy the simple things in life. Plant a garden, read the comics, stroll through the woods.

- ৡ Stay healthy; eat well; exercise. Keep an active body and mind.

There is no happiness; there is no misery; like that growing out of the dispositions which consecrate or desecrate a home.

—EDWIN H. CHAPIN

Resolve family quarrels.

Family disputes are normal, unavoidable, and even helpful. Family members often emerge from conflict with a clearer, stronger, and healthier sense of family unity and commitment. You can resolve conflict with a family member in a way that strengthens your relationship.

Yes, You Can!
⊱

- A necessary prerequisite to implementing the steps on this list is to swallow your pride and believe that your most important goal is to restore family harmony.

- Restore the dignity and self-respect of family members who may have lost face during the disagreement or who may lose face in the process of resolving the dispute. Applaud members who are willing to back down from earlier positions.

- Offer to make a concession. Give in on demands; make a friendly gesture. Welcome reciprocation.

- Admit you were wrong about something. This gesture is likely to encourage the other person to do the same. If so, the two of you may be on the road to reconciliation.

- Recognize that a lot of family conflict is caused not by genuine disagreement but by misunderstanding. Initiate a meeting where the two of you role-play each other, doing your best to articulate the position the *other person* has taken. Listen as your earlier miscommunications get cleared up.

- When confronting a family member, stick to the issues. Don't get caught up in an exchange of accusations.

- Focus on fixing the future, not laying blame for the past. Work together to arrive at an answer to the question "What do we need to do to have the kind of relationship we both want from now on?"

Love, the quest;
marriage, the conquest;
divorce, the inquest.

—HELEN ROWLAND

Cope with divorce.

About half of married couples will divorce sometime within the first seven years of marriage. Marriages of longer duration are also vulnerable. If your marriage breaks up, can you find happiness again and go on with your life?

Yes, You Can!
༬

- ❧ If you're losing sleep, suffering from depression, or enduring psychosomatic illness, get professional help.

- ❧ If you believe you still love your "ex," ask yourself if you are dreaming of a relationship that clearly will never again exist. It may be time to wake up and get on with your life.

- ❧ If children are involved, be as honest as possible with them about the breakup without criticizing their mother/father. Once you settle the basic conditions of the separation, tell the children what happened gently, honestly, and calmly without saying too much.

- ❧ Get feedback from others on how you're handling things. Are you being a problem solver or an avenger? Are you asserting your needs or are you being a patsy?

- ❧ Immerse yourself in constructive, energetic activities. Go to the gym, jogging track, tennis court, or swimming pool. Volunteer in the community; start a hobby; take on new work.

- ❧ View the divorce as the end of an unhappy chapter in your life and the beginning of a new one. Symbolize the transition in little ways by changing some aspect of your appearance or lifestyle, but don't go overboard.

- ❧ Write a story about what happened, and describe five things you learned about yourself that will help you to have stronger love relationships in the future.

- ❧ Don't be dragged into verbal battles with your "ex" on the telephone or in person. Say, "We'll continue this another time," and then hang up or leave.

Death is not the greatest loss in life. The greatest loss is what dies within us while we live.

—NORMAN COUSINS

Cope with the death of a loved one.

Following the death of someone close, many people feel that life has lost its meaning, and they convince themselves that they'll be miserable for the rest of their lives. You can successfully overcome these natural reactions.

Yes, You Can!

⤫

- ◈ Grieve naturally. Let yourself cry, both in public and in private. The sooner and more fully you can express your pain, the sooner you will be able to get on with your life.

- ◈ Expect to pass through several stages as your grieving progresses: shock, disbelief, denial, painful sadness, emptiness, anxiety, irritability, guilt, anger, and preoccupation with memories of the deceased.

- ◈ Express any anger you experience because the person has left you. If you feel, "Why did you do this to me?" don't be ashamed to shout it.

- ◈ Recognize that the person who left you would be upset at the thought that you intend to stop living. Think about the millions who have survived bereavement. Know that you will, too.

- ◈ Remember that you will always have your memories to keep this person alive in your heart. In this way, his or her powerful influence on you will *never* end.

- ◈ Talk to others who have faced loss, and ask them to share their experiences. Join or start a support group.

- ◈ If your faith includes a belief in life after death, keep in mind that heaven is a far better place for your loved one. Look forward to a reunion there.

- ◈ Be patient with yourself. Some people need time to recover. On the other hand, if you bounce back quickly, don't mistake this as a sign of not caring.

- ◈ As soon as you *think* you may need counseling, get it.

About the Authors

Sam Deep taught at the college level for twenty years, most recently in the communication department at the University of Pittsburgh, where he also served as an administrator. In 1986 he expanded his part-time consulting practice into a full-time career. He now helps organizations empower their employees by enhancing the interpersonal, communication, and leadership skills of their managers.

Lyle Sussman is Professor of Management in the School of Business at the University of Louisville, Kentucky. Previously he was affiliated with the University of Michigan and the University of Pittsburgh. He received his Ph.D. in communications and industrial relations from Purdue University. He serves on the faculties of several state and national banking schools.

Deep and Sussman conduct seminars and give speeches for a variety of organizations from the *Fortune* 500, the health industry, public school systems, colleges and universities, professional associations, and government agencies.

Their recent clients include: Alcoa, American Bankers Association, Austrian National Bank, Bahamas Ministry of Tourism, Blockbuster Video, Brown Williamson Corporation, Carnegie Mellon University, Deloitte & Touche, the Department of Veterans Affairs, General Electric, Hallmark Cards, Humana, Kentucky Fried Chicken, Ketchum Communications, Kraft Food

Service, McDonald's Corporation, Mellon Bank, Merck & Co., Miles Inc., National Cattleman's Association, the National Park Service, Paradise Island Resort and Casino, PPG, Pittsburgh Symphony, Presbyterian-University Hospital, Puerto Rico Hotel and Tourism Association, Rally's, Rockwell International, South-Western Bell, Union Switch & Signal, the U.S. Postal Service, Westinghouse, and Xerox.

Their ideas about leadership and communication have appeared in the *Chicago Tribune, Cosmopolitan, Self, USAir Magazine, Working Woman, Working Mother, Ladies Home Journal, Boardroom Reports,* and *Executive Report,* to name a few. Their taped programs appear on USAir's Inflight Audio Entertainment. They have been interviewed on countless radio and television programs throughout the United States and Canada. Their management columns have been carried by four newspapers. Their management best-seller *Smart Moves* has been published in eleven foreign languages.

Yes, You Can!—The Program

When was the last time you had a professional development experience that actually *involved* you—a program where you not only learned but also had fun? We have created a *Yes, You Can!* program called **Make It Happen!** It is unlike any other you have ever attended.

The *Yes, You Can!* program is not a spectator sport. You'll do more than take notes. You'll be a part of the action from beginning to end. You'll leave with commitments for how you will turn the program's ideas into plans to benefit both you and your organization.

Here's What Past Sponsors of Their Programs Have Said:
Few people come close to your style of excellence. Your professional expertise allowed you to become a master at capturing our audiences across the country.

>—Marquetta Glass, Manager of National Retail Training,
> Hallmark Cards

Excellent presentation! Informative and entertaining. Kept everyone's interest from start to finish. Provided me with useful information I could take to the job immediately.

>—Thomas Henrion, President and CEO,
> KFC Foodservice Purchasing Cooperative

Program Benefits

Sam Deep and Lyle Sussman will teach you how to:

§ Talk the talk and walk the walk, aligning your behavior with your values.

§ Turn positive thinking into positive action.

§ Communicate with greater confidence and clarity.

§ Understand and overcome resistance to change.

§ Improve your skills in resolving conflict and disagreements.

§ Give and receive constructive criticism.

§ Improve your listening skills.

§ Assess your strengths and weaknesses as a leader, follower, and team player.

§ Inspire employees, please bosses, encourage peers, and serve customers.

Who Should Attend

Managers and employees at any and all levels will benefit. Secretaries, sales representatives, engineers, accountants, teachers, bankers, government workers, communications specialists, marketing executives, health care professionals, and firstline supervisors through CEOs—all need to hear the *Yes, You Can!* message. Bring your entire team!

Program Lengths

The full program typically runs from 8:30 A.M. to 3:00 P.M. *Yes, You Can!* is also available as a shorter seminar or a ninety-minute dynamic keynote presentation, often retitled "12 Keys to Personal and Professional Success."

Presenters

You may request that either Sam Deep or Lyle Sussman, or both, conduct the full program. The keynote presentation is most often given by one or the other.

Contact

Call (412) 487-2379 to find out if the *Yes, You Can!* program is coming to your city soon or to arrange an in-house presentation.

You can also write to Sam Deep and Lyle Sussman at:
   Seminars by Sam Deep
   1920 Woodside Road
   Glenshaw, PA 15116

Other Seminars by Sam Deep and Lyle Sussman
Each of these seminars is carefully crafted in length and in focus to meet the needs of your organization or group.

- As Time Goes By
- Building Teams That Win
- Building a Unified Board
- Communicating with Confidence
- Criticism and Praise: Giving and Getting Them
- Dealing with Difficult Employees
- Doing More with Less
- Four Secrets of Leadership
- Helping Employees Give Great Customer Service
- Hiring Top Performers
- Leadership 2000
- Making Change Happen
- Making Meetings Work
- Presenting Yourself with Impact
- Selling Your Ideas to Others
- The Servant Leader
- Seven Secrets of Highly Effective CEOs
- The Smartest of Smart Moves for People in Charge
- Ten Habits of Exceptional Sales Professionals
- What to Say to Get What You Want
- You're Not Listening!

Other Useful Books by Sam Deep and Lyle Sussman

Smart Moves

This "Manager's Book of Lists" will show you the right moves for writing reports, resolving conflicts, budgeting time, and other on-the-job tasks, all in 140 checklists. "Packed with useful information" *(Denver Post)*
ISBN 0-201-51812-0   264 pages $11.00

Smart Moves for People in Charge

You face special responsibilities when you're in charge, whether you run a small business, a big department, or a growing corporation. The 130 checklists in this book will help you to be a better leader. "A handy reference tool" *(Cedar Rapids Gazette)*
ISBN 0-201-48328-9   320 pages $15.00

What to Say to Get What You Want

In this handbook for communications skills you'll find the "Ten Commandments of Change," plus tips for handling 44 types of bosses, employees, coworkers, and customers. "The simple rules for dealing with difficult people" *(Orange County Register)*
ISBN 0-201-57712-7   336 pages $9.95

All these books by Sam Deep and Lyle Sussman are available from bookstores or:

Order Department
Addison-Wesley Publishing Company
1 Jacob Way
Reading, MA 01867
(800) 358-4566